WINTER FUN. FROM "ST. NICHOLAS" MAGAZINE

Published @ 2017 Trieste Publishing Pty Ltd

ISBN 9780649734511

Winter Fun. From "St. Nicholas" Magazine by William O. Stoddard

Edited by Trieste Publishing Pty Ltd.
 Cover @ 2017

www.triestepublishing.com

WILLIAM O. STODDARD

WINTER FUN. FROM "ST. NICHOLAS" MAGAZINE

Trieste

WINTER FUN

FROM

"St. Nicholas" Magazine

BY

WILLIAM O. STODDARD

AUTHOR OF "DAB KINZER," "THE QUARTET," "SALTILLO
BOYS," ETC.

LONDON

BICKERS & SON, 1 LEICESTER SQUARE

. 1886

CONTENTS.

iv CONTENTS.

CONTENTS.

CHAPTER XVII.

CHAPTER XVIII.

CHAPTER XIX.

WINTER FUN.

WINTER FUN.

CHAPTER I.

ALL AROUND A FIREPLACE.

THE gate that opened from the yard into the lane
leading back to the barn was directly opposite the
side-door of the house. The door was shut, but the
gate was open; and in it stood a gray-haired dame
with a sharp nose and silver-rimmed spectacles. The
house behind her was a small one, white-painted,
without blinds to its windows, but with an air of
snug comfort all over it. Just beyond the gate and
the woman stood a tall, vigorous-looking young fellow
of not more than eighteen; and his left hand was on
the nose of a nice-looking horse; and behind the
horse was a neat, bright, very red cutter. The boy's
face was also somewhat rosy; and so, for that frosty
moment, was the tip of his mother's nose.

"Now, Lavawjer, that there cutter's all you've got
to show for about as hard a month's work as ever
you put in; but I won't say that the deacon drew a
hard bargain with ye."

"Well, mother, just look at it."

"I'm a-lookin' at it, and it isn't the cutter it was. You've had it painted red, and varnished, and you've put on a new goose-neck in place of the broken one, and there's room in it for two if neither one on 'em was too heavy."

"That's so, mother; and all you've got to do is just to try it. I'll take you to meeting in it next Sunday. You ought to see how the colt gets over the snow with only that cutter behind him."

"I ain't a bit sorry you've got somethin' for him to do. You've been a-raisin' on him since before he was a yearlin', and he hasn't earned his keep."

Mrs. Stebbins had made her first look at her son's new cutter a severe and searching one, and she told him very fully all her thoughts about it and about the sorrel colt. She was a faithful mother; but there was pride in her eye, and more red on the tip of her nose, when she turned to go into the house. He did not hear her say to herself, —

"He's the smartest boy in all Benton Valley, and now he's got the nicest horse and cutter, — that is, for his age, considerin', — and I ain't one bit afraid it'll spile him."

He was now leading his sorrel pet, with the jaunty cutter following, out through the lane to the barn. It was a grand thing, and out of the common range of human events, for a country-boy of his age to have

such an outfit all his own. Such things can always
be accounted for, when you find them happening.
If he were not just a little "spiled," it was no fault
of his mother. She was a widow, and he was her
only son; and she had talked to him and about him
pretty steadily from the day he was born. He looked
older than he really was now, and she often said so;
but she sometimes added that he knew enough for a
man of forty. She had named him "Le Voyageur,"
after a great French traveller whose name she had
seen in a book when she was a girl; but the Valley
boys had massacred all the beauty of it, and short-
ened it into "Vosh." No other fellow in all that
country had so very remarkable a nickname.

"Now, Jeff," he said, as he cast the sorrel loose
from the cutter, "maybe there's a chance a-coming
that you'll have a better-looking load to haul next
time you're hitched in. I'll want ye to show your
oats if you do."

That remark could hardly have referred to Mrs.
Stebbins and her next Sunday's ride to the meeting-
house; but Jeff whinnied gently in reply, as if to
express his willingness for any improvement, and
Vosh led him into the stable.

"City folks know some things," he remarked
to Jeff, while he poured some oats in the manger;
"but they don't know what good sleighing is.
We'll show 'em, soon as we get some bells; and

the deacon's got more buffaloes than he knows what to do with."

That was a good half-hour before supper, and he seemed in no hurry to get into the house; but it was odd that his mother, at the very same time, should have been talking to herself, in default of any other hearer, about "city folks" and their ways and by-ways and shortcomings. She seemed to know a great deal about them, and particularly about their general ignorance concerning snow, ice, cold weather, and all the really good things of genuine winter. Both she and her son evidently had kindly and liberal feelings towards the hardest kind of frost, and were free to say as much, but were in doubt as to whether city people could live and be comfortable in such weather as had already come. Beyond a doubt, they were waiting for somebody. There is nothing else in the wide world that will keep people talking as that will; and Mrs. Stebbins said some things that sounded as if she were asking questions of the teakettle.

Down the road a little distance, and on the other side of it, a very different pair of people were even more interested in city folk, and not in their short-comings so much as in the fact that certain of them seemed to be too long a-coming. They were away back in the great old-fashioned kitchen of a farm-house, as large as three of the one in which Mrs. Stebbins was getting supper for Vosh.

"Aunt Judith, I hear 'em!"

"Now, Pen, my child!"

The response came from the milk-room, and was followed by the clatter of an empty tin milk-pan falling on the floor.

"It sounded like bells."

"It's the wind, Pen. Sakes alive! but they ought to be here by this time."

"There, aunt Judith!"

Pen suddenly darted out of the kitchen, leaving the long hind-legs of a big pair of waffle-irons sticking helplessly out from the open door of the stove.

"Pen! Penelope!—I declare, she's gone. There, I've dropped another pan. What's got into me tonight? I just do want to see those children. Poor things, how froze they will be!"

Penelope was pressing her eager, excited little face close to the frost-flowers on the sitting-room window. It was of no use, cold as it made the tip of her nose, to strain her blue eyes across the snowy fields, or up the white, glistening reaches of the road. There was nothing like a sleigh in sight, nor did her sharpest listening bring her any sound of coming sleigh-bells.

"Pen! Penelope Farnham! What's that a-burnin'? Sakes alive! if she hasn't gone and stuck them waffle-irons in the fire! She's put a waffle in 'em too."

Yes, and the smoke of the lost waffle was carrying tales into the milk-room.

"O aunt Judith! I forgot. I just wanted to try one."

"Jest like you, Penelope Farnham. You're always a-tryin' somethin'. If you ain't a trial to me, I wouldn't say so. Now, don't you tetch them waffles once again, on no account."

"It's all burned as black " —

"Course it is, — black as a coal. I'd ha' thought you'd ha' known better'n that. Why, when I was ten years old I could ha' cooked for a fam'ly."

"Guess I could do that," said Pen resolutely; but aunt Judith was shaking out the smoking remains of the spoiled waffle into the "pig-pail," and curtly responded, —

"That looks like it. You'll burn up the irons yet."

Half a minute of silence followed, and then she again spoke from the milk-room : —

"Penelope, look at the sittin'-room fire, and see if it wants any more wood on it. They'll be chilled clean through when they git here."

Pen obeyed; but it only needed one glance into the great roaring fireplace to make sure that no kind of chill could keep its hold on anybody in the vicinity of that blaze.

A stove was handier to cook by, and therefore

Mr. Farnham had put aside his old-fashioned notions, to the extent of having one set up in the
kitchen. The parlor too, he said, belonged to his
wife more than it did to him, and therefore he had
yielded again, and there was a stove there also. It
was hard at work now. He had insisted, however,
that the wide, low-ceilinged, comfortable sitting-room
should remain a good deal as his father had left it to
him ; and there the fireplace held its wood-devouring
own. That was one reason why it was the pleasantest
room in the house, especially on a winter evening.

Penelope had known that fireplace a long while.
She had even played " hide-and-coop " in it in warm
weather, when it was bright and clean. But she
thought she had never before seen it so full. " Such
a big back-log!" she exclaimed aloud. But aunt
Judith had followed her in to make sure of the condition of things, and it was her voice that added, —

"Yes, and the fore-stick's a foot through. Your
father heaped it up just before he set out for the
village. He might a'most as well have piled the
whole tree in."

"Father likes fire: so do I."

"He's an awful wasteful man with his wood,
though. Pen, just you put down that poker. Do
you want to have them there top logs a-rollin' across
the floor ? "

"That one lies crooked."

"My child! let it be. I daresn't leave you alone one minute. You'll burn the house down over our heads, one of these days."

Pen obeyed. She slowly lowered the long, heavy iron rod, and laid it down on the hearth; but such a fire as that was a terrible temptation. Almost any man in the world might have been glad to have a good poke at it, if only to see the showers of sparks go up from the glowing hickory logs.

"There they come!"

Pen turned away from the fire very suddenly; and aunt Judith put her hand to her ear, and took off her spectacles, so she could listen better.

"I shouldn't wonder."

"That's the sleigh-bells! It's our sleigh, I know it is. Shall I begin to make the waffles?"

"Don't you tetch 'em. Pen, get out that chiny thing your mother got to put the maple-sirup in."

"Oh, I forgot that."

She brought it out like a flash now; and it must have been the only thing she had forgotten when she set the table, for she had walked anxiously around it twenty times, at least, since she put the last plate in its place.

Faint and far, from away down the road, beyond the turn, the winter wind brought up the merry jingle of bells. By the time Pen had brought the china pitcher for the sirup from its shelf in the closet, and once more darted to the window, she could see her father's black team — blacker than ever against the snow — trotting towards the house magnificently.

"Don't I wish I'd gone with 'em! But it was Corry's turn. I guess Susie isn't used to waffles, but she can't help liking 'em."

That was quite possible, but it might also be of some importance whether Penelope or aunt Judith should have the care of the waffle-irons.

Jingle-jangle-jingle, louder and louder, came the merry bells, till they stopped at the great gate, and a tall boy sprang out of the sleigh to open it. The front-door of the house swung open quicker than did the gate, and Pen was on the stoop, shouting anxiously, —

"Did they come, Corry? Did you get 'em?"

A deep voice from the sleigh responded with a chuckle, —

"Yes, Pen, we caught 'em both. They're right here, and they can't get away now."

"I see 'em! There's cousin Susie!"

At that moment she remembered to turn and shout back into the house, —

"Aunt Judith, here they are! They've got 'em both!"

But there was her aunt already in the doorway, with the steaming waffle-irons in one hand.

"Sakes alive, child! You'll freeze the whole house. Poor things! and they ain't used to cold weather."

Aunt Judith must have had an idea that it was generally summer in the city.

The sleigh jangled right up to the bottom step of the stoop now. Mr. Farnham got out first, and was followed by his wife. They were followed by a very much wrapped-up young lady, into whose arms Pen fairly jumped, exclaiming, —

"Susie! Susie Hudson!"

There were no signs of frost-bite on Susie's rosy cheeks, and she hugged Penelope vigorously. Just behind her, a little more dignifiedly, there descended from the sleigh a boy who may have been two years younger, say fourteen or fifteen, who evidently felt that the occasion called upon him for his self-possession.

"Pen," said her mother, "don't you mean to kiss cousin Porter?"

Pen was ready. Her little hands went out, and her bright, welcoming face was lifted for the kiss; but, if Porter Hudson had been a waffle, he would not have been burned by it at all. It was not altogether because he was a boy, and a big one, but that he was more a stranger. Susie had paid her country-cousins a long summer visit only the year before, while Porter had not been seen by any of them since he was four years old. Both he and they had forgotten that he had ever been so small as that.

Mr. Farnham started for the barn, to put away his team, bidding Corry go on into the house with his cousins. Aunt Judith was at last able to close the door behind them, and keep any more of the winter from coming in.

It took but half a minute to help Susie and Porter Hudson get their things off, and then aunt Judith all but forced them into the chairs she had set for them in front of the great fireplace.

"What a splendid fire !"

It was Susie said that, with the glow of it making her very pretty face look brighter and prettier, and very happy. She had already won aunt Judith's heart over again by being so glad to see her, and she kept right on winning it, needlessly ; for every thing about that room had to be looked at twice, and admired, and told how nice it was.

"It is indeed a remarkably fine fire," said Porter with emphasis, at the end of a full minute.

"And we're going to have waffles and maple-sugar for supper," said Pen. "Don't you like waffles ?"

"Yes," said Porter : "they're very nice, no doubt."

"And after such a sleigh-ride," chimed in Susie. "The sleighing is splendid, beautiful !"

"More snow here than you have in the city?" suggested Corry to Porter.

"Yes, a little; but then, we have to have ours removed as fast as it comes down, — get it out of the way, you know."

"It isn't in the way here. We'd have a high time of it if we tried to get rid of our snow."

"I should say you would. And then it does very well where the people make use of sleighs."

"Don't you have 'em in the city?"

Pen was looking at her cousins with eyes that were full of pity, but at that moment aunt Judith called to her from the kitchen, —

"Penelope, come and watch the waffle-irons while I make the tea."

"Waffles!" exclaimed Susie. "I never saw any made."

"Come with me, then. I'll show you; that is, if you're warm enough."

"Warm! Why, I wasn't cold one bit. I'm warm as toast."

Out they went; and there were so many errands on the hands of aunt Judith and Mrs. Farnham just then, that the girls had the kitchen stove to themselves for a few moments. Pen may have been six years younger, but she was conscious of a feeling of immense superiority in her capacity of cook. She kept it until, as she was going over, for Susie's benefit, a list of her neighbors, and telling what had become of them since the summer visit, Mr. Farnham came in at the kitchen-door, and almost instantly exclaimed, —

"Mind your waffles, Pen. You're burning 'em."

"Why, so I did, — that one, just a little. I was telling Susie" —

"A little, my child!" interrupted aunt Judith. "I'd as lief eat burnt leather. Oh, dear! give me those irons."

"Now, aunt Judith, please fill 'em up for Susie to try. I want to show her how."

The look on Susie's face was quite enough to keep aunt Judith from making a breath of objection, and the rich creamy batter was poured into the smoking moulds.

"Don't you let it burn, Susie," said Pen. "They want to come out when they're just a good brown. I'll show you."

Susie set out to watch the fate of that waffle most diligently; but she had not at all counted on what might come in the mean time, — a visitor, for instance.

Susie had already asked about the Stebbinses, and Pen had answered, —

"They know you're coming. Vosh was here this very morning, and I told him; and he said he'd be glad to have you call and see him."

"Call and see him ? Well."

No more remarks had room to be made in just then; for, only a few minutes before aunt Judith poured out that waffle, Mrs. Stebbins had said to her son, —

"I heered the deacon's sleigh come up the road, Lavawjer. Jest you take a teacup, and go over and borry a drawin' of tea of Miss Farnham. Don't you miss nothin'. City ways'll spile most anybody; and that there Hudson gal — Susie, her name was — is likely gettin' stuck up enough by this time."

She told him a great deal more than that before he got out of the door with his teacup, and it looked as if he were likely to have questions to answer when he should come back.

He escaped a little unceremoniously, right in the middle of a long sentence. And so, just when Susie was most deeply absorbed in her experiment, there came a loud rap at the kitchen-door; then, without waiting for any one to come and open it, the door swung back, and in walked Vosh, as large as life, with the teacup in his hand.

He did look large; but no amount of frost or fire could have made him color so red as he did when Susie Hudson let go of the irons, and stepped right forward to shake hands with him.

"How d'ye do, Vosh ? How is your mother ?"

"Pretty well, thank you. How do you do ? Mother's first-rate, but she's wrong this time. I don't see as you're stuck up a bit. You're just like you was last summer, only prettier."

The one great weakness in the character of Vosh Stebbins was that he could not help telling the truth, to save his life. It was very bad for him sometimes; and now, before Susie could smother her laugh, and make up her mind what to answer him, he held out his teacup to aunt Judith.

"Miss Farnham, mother told me to borrow a drawing of tea. We ain't out of tea, by a long ways; but she heard the deacon's sleigh a-coming, and she wanted to know if the folks from the city'd got here."

"They've come," said aunt Judith shortly, "Susie and her brother. You tell your mother I wish she'd send me over a dozen of eggs. The skunks have stolen ours as fast as the hens have laid 'em."

"We've got some," said Vosh. "I'll fetch 'em over. — Susie, where's your brother?"

"He's in the sitting-room."

"Yes, Vosh," said Pen, "he's there. Walk right in. Corry's there too, and mother, and — O Susie! Dear me! our waffle's burned again."

"Why! so it is."

"Never mind, Susie," said aunt Judith with the most hospitable recklessness, as she shook out the proceeds of that careless cookery upon a plate. "It's only spiled on one side. There's always some of 'em get burned. Some folks like 'em better when they're kind o' crisp. I'll fill ye up another."

Vosh looked as if he would willingly stay and see how the next trial succeeded; but politeness required him to walk on into the sitting-room, and be introduced to Porter Hudson.

"Vosh," said Corry, "he's never been in the country in winter before in all his life, and he's come to stay ever so long. So's Susie."

"That's good," began Vosh; but he was interrupted by an invitation from Mrs. Farnham to stay to supper, and eat some waffles, and he very promptly replied, —

"Thank you, I don't care if I do. I threw our waffle-irons at Bill Hinks's dog one day last fall. It most killed him, but it busted the irons, and we've been 'tending to have 'em mended ever sence. We haven't done it yet, though, and so we haven't had any waffles."

Aunt Judith had now taken hold of the business at the kitchen stove; for Susie had made one triumphant success, and she might not do as well next time. All the rest were summoned to the supper-table.

The room was all one glow of light and warmth. The maple-sugar had been melted to the exact degree of richness required. The waffles were coming in rapidly and in perfect condition. Everybody had been hungry, and felt more so now; and even Porter Hudson was compelled to confess that the first supper of his winter visit in the country was at least equal to any he could remember eating anywhere.

"City folks," remarked Penelope, "don't know how to cook waffles, but I'll teach Susie. Then she can make 'em for you when you go back, only you can't do it without milk and eggs."

"We can buy 'em."

"Of course you can; but we lay our own eggs, only they get stole. You'll have to send up here for your maple-sugar."

"We can buy that too, I guess."

"But we get it right out of the woods. You just ought to be here in sugar-time."

"Pen," said her father, "we're going to keep 'em both till then, and make them ever so sweet before we let 'em go home."

He was at that moment glancing rapidly from one to another of those four fresh young faces. He did not tell them so, but he was tracing that very curious and shadowy thing which we call "a family resemblance." It was there, widely as the faces varied otherwise; and all their years had not taken it out of the older faces. Perhaps the city cousins, with especial help from Susie rather than Porter, had somewhat the advantage in good looks. They had it in dress also; but when it came to names — well, aunt Judith herself had had the naming of her brother's children, and she had done her best by them. Penelope and Coriolanus were every way larger names than Porter and Susan; and Vosh could have told them that there is a great deal in a name, if you can get it well boiled down for every-day use.

CHAPTER II.

VOSH STEBBINS hurried away from Deacon Farnham's pretty soon after supper, but he had made no
sort of mistake in staying that long. He had understood his duty to his mother precisely, and he had
done it to her entire satisfaction. Almost her first
words, after his return home, were, —

"Made ye stay to tea, did they? Well, I wouldn't
have had ye not to stay, for any thing. Susie's
fetched along her brother with her, has she? Now,
jest you sit right down, and tell me; and I won't
say one word till you git through, and I want to
know."

"Miss Farnham wants a dozen of eggs."

"You don't say! Well, you jest take 'em right
over, but don't you wait a minute. They won't want
ye 'round the first evening. Tell her our poultry's
doin' first-rate, and I don't see why she doesn't ever
have any kind of luck with winter layin'. She doesn't

19

manage right, somehow. Tell her it's all in feedin'
of 'em. No kind of hens'll do well onless they git
somethin' to eat."

Vosh was counting his eggs into a basket, thirteen
to the dozen; and he was out of the door with them
before his mother had said half she wished to say
about the best method for making hens prosper in
cold weather. He obeyed his orders excellently,
however, and came back at once to make his report
to his mother as to the results of his first visit; that
is, he returned to sit still, and put in a few words
here and there, while she told him all he had done
and said, and a good deal more than he had said or
done, at Deacon Farnham's tea-table.

It looked at last as if Mrs. Stebbins could almost
have gone right on with an account of what was yet
doing and saying around the great fire in the sitting-
room. Vosh loved his mother dearly; but he was
all the while thinking of that other fireplace, and
wishing he were there — not in it, of course, but
sitting in front of it.

There was indeed a great deal of merry talk
going on there, but Mrs. Farnham was a considerate
woman. She insisted upon it that her niece and
nephew must be tired with their long journey, and
that they should go to bed in good season. It was
of little use for them to assert the contrary, and
Susie knew more about country hours than her

brother did. The sitting-room had to be given up, fire and all, in favor of sleep.

The last words Porter Hudson heard anybody say that night came from the lips of Penelope : —

"You needn't wait for me to ring the second bell in the morning. You'd a good deal better come right down into the sitting-room, where it's warm."

It had taken three generations of hard-working and well-to-do Farnhams to build all there was of that great, queer, rambling, comfortable old farmhouse. Each owner had added something on one side or the other, or in the rear ; so that there was now room enough in it for the largest kind of a family. Porter Hudson now had a good-sized chamber all to himself ; but he remarked of it, shortly after he got in, —

"No furnace heaters in this house ; of course not : they don't have such things in the country."

No : nor was there any gas, nor hot and cold water ; and the furniture was only just as much as was really needed. He had never before slept in a feather-bed ; but he was not at all sorry to burrow into one that night, out of the pitilessly frosty air of that chamber.

"How a fellow does go down !" he said to himself ; "and it fits all around him. I'll be warm in a minute." And so he was, and with the warmth came the soundest kind of slumber. The Farnhams had kept any number of geese, year after year, in earlier days, and all their feather-beds were uncommonly deep and liberal.

Susie had Pen for a chum, and that was a good reason why neither of them fell asleep right away. It is always a wonder how much talking there is to be done. It is a good thing, too, that so many enterprising people, old and young, are always ready to take up the task of talking it, even if they have to lie awake for a while.

Silence came at last, creeping from room to room; and there is hardly anywhere else such perfect silence to be obtained as can be had in and about a farmhouse away up country, in the dead of winter and the dead of night. It is so still that you can almost hear the starlight crackle on the snow, if there is no wind blowing.

Winter mornings do not anywhere get up as early as men and women are compelled to, but it is more completely so on a farm than in the city. The chamber Porter Hudson slept in was as dark as a pocket when he heard the clang of Penelope's first bell that next morning after his arrival. He sprang out of bed at once, and found his candle, and lighted it to dress by. One glance through the frosty windows told him how little was to be seen at that time of the year and of the day.

In another instant all his thoughts went down

stairs ahead of him, and centred themselves upon the great fireplace in the sitting-room. He dressed himself with remarkable quickness, and followed them. He thought that he had never in his life seen a finer-looking fire, the moment he was able to spread his hands in front of it.

Mrs. Farnham was there too, setting the breakfast-table, and smiling on him; and Porter's next idea was, that his aunt was the rosiest, pleasantest, and most comfortable of women.

" It would take a good deal of cold weather to freeze her," he said to himself; and he was right.

He could hear aunt Judith out in the kitchen, complaining to Susie and Pen that every thing in the milk-room had frozen. When Corry and his father came in from feeding the stock, however, they both declared that it was a "splendid, frosty, nipping kind of a morning." They looked as if it might be, and Porter hitched his chair a little nearer the fire; but Corry added, —

" Now, Port, we're in for some fun."

" All right. What is it ? "

" We're going to the woods after breakfast. You and I'll take our guns with us, and see if we can't knock over some rabbits."

" Shoot some rabbits ! "

" I'll take father's gun, and you can take mine."

Just then Pen's voice sounded from the kitchen excitedly, —

"Do you hear that, Susie? They're going to the woods. Let's go!"

"Oh! if they'll let us."

"Course they will."

"Pen! Penelope Farnham! Look out for those cakes."

"I'm turning 'em, aunt Judith. I'm doing 'em splendidly. — Susie, some of your sausages are a'most done. Let me take 'em out for you."

"No, Pen: I want to cook them all myself. You 'tend to your cakes."

Buckwheat-cakes and home-made sausages, — what a breakfast that was for a frosty morning!

Susie Hudson was puzzled to say which she enjoyed most, — the cooking or the eating; and she certainly did her share of both very well for a young lady of sixteen from the great city.

"Port, can you shoot?" asked Corry a little suddenly at table.

"Shoot! I should say so. Do you ever get any thing bigger than rabbits out here?"

"Didn't you know? Why, right back from where we're going this morning are the mountains. Not a farm till you get away out into the St. Lawrence-river country."

"Yes, I know all that."

"Sometimes the deer come right down, specially in winter. Last winter there was a bear came down and stole one of our hogs, but we got him."

"Got the hog back? Wasn't he hurt?"

"Hurt! Guess he was. The bear killed him. But we followed the bear, and we got him, — Vosh Stebbins and father and me."

Porter tried hard to look as if he were quite accustomed to following and killing all the bears that meddled with his hogs; but Pen exclaimed, —

"Now, Susie, you needn't be scared a bit. There won't be a single bear — not where you're going."

"Won't there?" said Susie almost regretfully. "How I'd like to see one!"

There was a great deal more to be said about bears and other wild creatures; and, just as breakfast was over, there came a great noise of rattling and creaking and shouting in front of the sitting-room windows.

"There he is!" said Corry.

Susie and her brother hurried to look; and there was Vosh Stebbins with Deacon Farnham's great wood-sleigh, drawn by two pairs of strong, long-horned, placid-looking oxen.

"Couldn't one pair draw it?" asked Porter of Corry.

"Guess they could, but two's easier; and, besides, they've nothing else to do. We'll heap it up too. You just wait and see."

There was not long to wait, for the excitement rose fast in the sitting-room, and Susie and Pen were

in that sleigh a little in advance of everybody else.
Its driver stood by the heads of his first yoke of oxen,
and Susie at once exclaimed, —

"Good - morning, Vosh.   What a tremendous
whip ! "

"Why, Susie," said Pen, "that isn't a whip, it's
an ox-gad."

"That's it, Pen," said Vosh ; but he seemed disposed to talk to his oxen rather than to anybody else.
The yoke next the sleigh stood on either side of a
long, heavy "tongue ;" but the foremost pair were
fastened to the end of that by a chain which passed
between them to a hook in their yoke.   These latter
two animals, as Vosh explained to Susie, "were only
about half educated, and they took more than their
share of driving."

He began to do it for them now, and it was half
a wonder to see how accurately the huge beasts kept
the right track down through the gate and out into
the road.   It seemed easier then, for all they had to
do was to go straight ahead.

"Let me take the whip, do, please," said Susie ;
and Vosh only remarked, as he handed it to her, —

"Guess you'll find it heavy."

She lifted it with both hands ; and he smiled all
over his broad, ruddy face, as she made a desperate
effort to swing the lash over the oxen.

"Go 'long now !   Git ap !   Cluck-cluck."

She chirruped to those oxen with all her might, while Vosh put his handkerchief over his mouth, and had a violent fit of coughing.

"You'll do !" shouted her uncle from behind the sleigh. "That's first-rate. I'll hire you to team it for me all the rest of the winter. — Boys, you'd better put down your guns. Lay them flat, and don't step on 'em."

Porter Hudson had stuck to his gun manfully from the moment it was handed him. He had carried it over his shoulder, slanting it a little across towards the other shoulder. He had seen whole regiments of city soldiers do that, and so he knew it was the correct way to carry a gun. He was now quite willing, however, to imitate Corry, and put his weapon down flat on the bottom of the sleigh. The gun would be safe there ; and, besides, he had been watching Vosh Stebbins, and listening, and he had an idea it was time he should show what he knew about oxen. They were plodding along very well, and Susie was letting them alone at the moment.

"Susie," he said, "give me that gad."

Vosh looked somewhat doubtful as she surrendered the whip. They were going up a little ascent, and right beyond them the fences on either side of the road seemed to stop. Beyond that, all was forest, and the road had a crooked look as it went in among the trees.

Porter had stronger arms than his sister, and he could do more with an ox-gad. The first swing he gave the long hickory stock, the heavy, far-reaching lash at the end of it came around with a "swish," and knocked the coon-skin cap from the head of Vosh. Then the whip came down — stock, lash, and all — along the broad backs of the oxen.

"Gee! Haw! G'lang! Get up! G'lang now! Haw! Gee!"

Porter felt that his reputation was at stake. He raised the gad again, and he shouted vigorously. The tongue-yoke of oxen right under his nose did not seem to mind it much, and plodded right along as if they had not heard any one say a word to them; but their younger and more skittish helpers in front shook their heads a little uneasily.

"Gee! Haw! G'lang!"

Porter was quite proud of the way the lash came down that time, and the cracker of it caught the near ox of the forward team smartly on the left ear. It was a complete success, undoubtedly; but, to Porter's astonishment, that bewildered yoke of steers forward whirled suddenly to the right. The next moment they were floundering in a snow-drift, as if they were trying to turn around and look at him.

Perhaps they were; but Vosh at that moment snatched the gad from Porter, and sprang out of the sleigh, saying something, as he went, about "not wanting to have the gals upset." Corry was dancing a sort of double shuffle, and shouting, —

"That's it! First time I ever saw an ox-team gee and haw together. Hurrah for you, Port!"

"Pen," said Susie, "what does he mean?"

"Mean? Don't you know? Why, it's 'gee' to turn 'em this way, and it's 'haw' to turn 'em that way. They can't turn both ways at once."

That double team had set out to do it quite obediently, but Vosh got matters straightened very quickly. Then he stuck to his whip and did his own driving, until the sleigh was pulled out of the road, half a mile farther, into a sort of open space in the forest. There was not much depth of snow on the ground, and there were stumps of trees sticking up through it in all directions. Vosh drove right on until he halted his team by a great pile of logs that were already cut for hauling.

"Are they not too big for the fireplace?" asked Susie of Pen.

"Of course they are," said Pen; but Corry added, —

"We can cut up all we want for the stoves after we get 'em to the house. The big ones'll cut in two for back-logs."

He had been telling Porter, all the way, about the fun there was in felling big trees, and that young gentleman had frankly proposed to cut down a few before they set out after any rabbits or bears.

"Just see father swing that axe!" said Pen proudly, as the stalwart old farmer walked up to a tall hickory, and began to make the chips fly.

"It's splendid!" said Susie.

Vosh Stebbins had his axe out of the sleigh now, and seemed determined to show what he could do.

It looked like the easiest thing in the world. He and the deacon merely swung their axes up, and let them go down exactly in the right place; and the glittering edges went in, in, with a hollow thud, and at every other cut a great chip would spring away across the snow.

"It doesn't take either of them a great while to bring a tree down," said Corry. "You fetch along that other axe, and we'll try one. They've all got to come down: so it doesn't make any difference what we cut into."

The girls were contented to stay in the sleigh and look on, and the oxen stood as still as if they intended never to move again.

"Susie!" exclaimed Pen, "here comes Ponto. Nobody knew where he was when we started."

There he was now, however, — the great shaggy, long-legged house-dog, — coming up the road with a succession of short, sharp barks, as if he were protesting against being left out of such a picnic-party as that.

" Pen ! he's coming right into the sleigh."

" No, he ain't. You'll see. He'll go after Corry.
He's only smelling to see if the guns are here. He
knows what they mean."

" Will he hunt ?"

" I guess he will. When father or Corry or Vosh
won't go, he goes off and hunts by himself, only he
doesn't bring home any game."

He seemed just now to be stirred to a sort of
frenzy of delighted barking by what his nose told
him, but at the end of it he sat down on the snow
near the sleigh. No dog of good common sense
would follow a boy with an axe away from the place
where the guns were.

Meantime, Corry had picked out a maple-tree of
medium size, and had cut a few chips from it. It
was easy to see that he knew how to handle an axe,
if he could not bury one as deeply in the wood of a
tree as could his father or Vosh. He also knew
enough too, somehow, to get well out of the way
when he handed the axe to Porter Hudson, remarking, —

" Now, Port, cut it right down. Maybe it's a bee-
tree."

" Bee-tree ! Are there any in winter ? Do you
ever find any ? "

" Well, not all the while ; but there are bee-trees,
and the bees must be in 'em, just the same, in any
kind of weather."

That was so, no doubt; but if there had been a dozen hives of bees hidden away in the solid wood of that vigorous maple-tree, they would have been safe there until spring, for all the chopping of Porter Hudson. He managed to make the edge of the axe hit squarely the first time it struck, but it did not more than go through the bark. No scratch like that would get a chip ready. Porter colored with vexation; and he gave his next cut a little hastily, but he gave it with all his might. The edge of the axe hit several inches from the first scratch, and it seemed to take a quick twist on its own account just as it struck. It glanced from the tree, and away it went into the snow, jerking its handle rudely out of Porter's hands.

"I declare!"

"I say, Port, don't let's cut down any more trees. Let's get our guns, and go down into the swamp for some rabbits. There's Ponto. He'll stir 'em up for us."

Porter was fishing for his axe with a pretty red face, and he replied, —

"I guess we'd better. I'm not much used to chopping."

"Of course not."

"We burn coal in the city."

"No chopping to do. I know how it is. Got your axe? Come on."

All that was very polite; but Corry had less trouble now, in keeping up a feeling of equality with his city cousin. They were nearly of an age; but a city boy of fourteen has seen a great many things that one of the same years, brought up among the northern lakes and mountains, knows nothing about, and Corry had been a little in awe of Porter.

They had tucked their trousers into their boots when they left the house; and now they got their guns out of the sleigh, slung their powder-flasks and shot-pouches over their shoulders, and marched away through the woods.

The two girls looked after them as if they also were hungry for a rabbit-hunt. As for Ponto, that very shaggy and snowy dog was plainly intending to run between every two trees, and through each and every clump of bushes, as if in a desperate state of dread lest he might miss the tracks of some game or other. Sniff, sniff, sniff, everywhere! and twice he actually began to paw the snow before he and his two sportsmen were out of sight from the sleigh.

"Boys can have more fun in the woods than girls," began Susie half regretfully.

"No, they can't, Susie. Just you watch that tree. It'll come down pretty quickly. It'll make the splendidest kind of a crash."

It was good fun to watch that chopping, and see the chips fly. Susie found herself becoming more

and more deeply interested, as the wide notches
sank farther and farther into the massive trunks of
the two trees her uncle and Vosh Stebbins were
working on. Vosh chopped for dear life; but, in
spite of all he could do, the deacon had his tree
down first. It was a tall, noble-looking tree. There
were no branches near the ground, but there was a
fine broad crown of them away up there where the
sun could get at them in summer. It seemed almost
a pity to destroy a forest-king like that, but at last
it began to totter and lean.

"O Pen! it's coming."

"Don't shut your eyes, Susie: keep 'em open, and
see it come."

Susie did try; but when that tall, majestic trunk
seemed to throw out its great arms, and give the
matter up, she could not look any longer, and she
put her head down. Then she heard a tremendous
dull, crashing sound, and her eyes came open to see
a cloud of light snow rising from the spot on which
the forest-king had fallen.

"Isn't it splendid!"

"Yes, Pen, it's wonderful."

"Vosh's tree is almost ready. There! it's going
to go."

Vosh had not been as careful as Deacon Farnham
in aiming the fall of his tree, for it went down into
the arms of a smaller one, crashing and breaking

through them ; and the sharp, snapping sound of the crushed branches went far and wide through the silence of the snowy forest.

Pen said nothing, and Susie was conscious of a sort of still feeling, as if she had no further remarks to make just then.

CHAPTER III.

THE RABBIT-HUNT.

DEACON FARNHAM was fond of chopping down trees; but he had not brought a big sleigh into the woods that morning, with two yoke of oxen, merely to have them stand still in the snow while he did some chopping. Such fires as he kept up at the farmhouse called for liberal supplies; and so Susie was to have an opportunity to see a load of logs put on.

She and Pen had to get out of the sleigh, and then she expressed her wonder if her uncle and Vosh would be strong enough to lift those huge "back-log" pieces into it:—

"They never can do it, Pen, not in all the world."

"Lift 'em! Of course they won't. I'll show you how they do it: it's dreadful easy, soon as you know how."

It would hardly have been as easy for Pen and Susie as it seemed to be for Vosh and the deacon.

They took all the side-stakes out of the sleigh, on

the side towards the wood-pile; and they put down, with one end of each on the sleigh, and the other end in the snow, a pair of long, strong pieces of wood that Vosh called "skids:" that made an inclined plane, and it was nothing but good hard work to roll the logs up, and into their places on the sleigh. They made a tier all over the sleigh-bottom, and then the lighter logs were piled on them in regular order, till the load was finished off on top with a heap of bark and brushwood.

"That'll crackle good when it burns," said Vosh. "I like brush on a fire: don't you?"

Susie said she did; and she probably told the truth, for she was beginning to think she liked every thing in the country, even in winter.

"Now, Pen," said Vosh, "if you and Susie'll climb up, we'll set out for home with this load."

"Isn't your father coming, Pen?"

"No, Susie, I guess he won't."

"Will he stay here and chop trees all alone?"

"He says he likes it, and he isn't a bit afraid of being alone. There's a man at the house to help Vosh when we get there. Now, Susie, we must climb."

There was fun in that, but Pen was up first.

"Is your dress caught, Susie? — Vosh, help Susie: she's caught on a splinter."

"I'll help her."

"No, you needn't. There, it isn't torn much. — Now, Pen, do you think the oxen can pull such a load as this?"

"Of course they can."

In a minute or so more, Susie began to have new ideas about the management of oxen, and how strong they were, and how wonderfully willing. They seemed to know exactly what to do, with a little help from Vosh and his long whip. When all was ready, and they bowed their horns, and strained against their yokes with their powerful necks, it seemed as if they could have moved any thing in the world.

One long strain, a creaking sound, and then a sudden giving-way and starting, and the snow began to crunch, crunch, beneath the wide, smooth runners of the sleigh. Vosh walked beside his team, and drove it away around in a semicircle, carefully avoiding trees and stumps, until he and his load were once more in the road, and on their way home.

"Hark!" exclaimed Susie just then. "Was that the report of a gun, or was it the sound of another tree falling?"

"Guess it was a gun," said Vosh. "It's one of the boys shooting at something. Plenty of game, if they can hit it."

If they had been listening with any kind of attention, they might have heard a similar sound before, although the place where the boys were was at some distance from what Vosh called "the clearing."

Corry and Porter had pushed on after Ponto as best they could; but he had not stirred up for them any game in the thick, gloomy forest.

"No rabbits here," said Porter.

"Sometimes there are a few," said Corry; "but this isn't the place. We're most there now: we'd better load up."

"The guns, — aren't they loaded?"

"No. We never leave a charge in. Father says a gun's always safe when it's empty."

Corry put the butt of his gun on the ground while he spoke, and Porter watched him narrowly.

"That's his powder-flask," he said to himself. "I might have known that much. The powder goes in first: of course it does."

He had never loaded a gun in all his life, and his experience with the axe had made him feel a little cautious. Still he tried to make quick work of it; and, when Corry began to push down a wad of paper after the powder, his city cousin did the same thing, only he was a little behindhand, and he put in a much bigger wad of paper.

"How he does ram it! So will I," Porter remarked.

"Don't put too many shot into that gun. I'll

measure 'em for you. You'll know next time. It scatters too much if you overcharge it."

Porter was wondering at that very moment how many shot he had better put in, or whether he should try the big shot from one side of his shot-pouch, or the smaller shot from the other.

" What are the big ones for ?" he asked, when he saw Corry choose the smaller size.

"Buckshot? Oh! you can kill almost any thing with buckshot, — deer, or even bear."

"Can you? I never used 'em. Thought they were big for rabbits."

He was glad to know his gun was correctly loaded, however; and he imitated Corry in putting on the caps for both barrels, as if he had served a long apprenticeship at that very business.

"We haven't reached the swamp yet, have we?"

"No, but we have a'most. It's a great place for rabbits, when you get there. Halloo! Ponto's started one! Come on, Port!"

They did not really need to stir a foot, for the swift little animal the dog had disturbed from his seat among the bushes was running his best right toward them.

"There he is!" shouted Porter.

"Try him, Port."

"No, you try him."

Corry's gun was at his shoulder, and in another second the bright flash leaped from the muzzle.

"Did you hit him? He didn't stop running: he kept right on."

"Missed him, I guess. Too many trees, and it was a pretty long shot."

"Why, it didn't seem far."

"Didn't it? That's 'cause it was over the snow: it was more'n ten rods. Hark! hear Ponto!"

The old dog was barking as if for dear life, and the boys ran as fast as the snow would let them. They had not far to go before they could see Ponto dancing around the foot of a huge beech-tree.

"If he hasn't treed him!"

"Treed a rabbit! Why, do you mean they can climb?"

"Climb! Rabbits climb! I guess not. But that tree's hollow. See that hole at the bottom? The rabbit's in there, sure."

"Can we get him?"

"We'll try, but it won't pay if it takes too long, — just one rabbit."

Porter Hudson had a feeling that it would be worth almost any thing in the world to catch that rabbit. He hardly knew how to go to work for it; but he felt very warm indeed while his cousin stooped down and poked his arm deeper and deeper into the hole in the tree. It did not go down, but up; and it was a pretty big one at its outer opening.

"Is it a hollow tree, Corry?"

"Guess not, only a little way up."

"Can you feel him?"

"Arm isn't long enough."

Ponto whimpered, very much as if he understood what his master was saying. That was probably not the first runaway game which had disappointed him by getting into a den of safety of one kind or another.

"Hey, Port! Here he comes!"

"Got him, have you?"

"There he is."

Corry withdrew his arm as he spoke, and held up in triumph a very large, fat, white rabbit.

"You did reach him."

"No, I didn't. Some of my shot had hit him, and he came down the hole of his own weight. Don't you see? They didn't strike him in the right place to tumble him right over: he could run."

"Poor fellow!" said Porter: "he won't run any more now."

It was of small use to pity that rabbit, when the one thought uppermost in his mind was that he could not go home happy unless he could carry with him another of the same sort, and of his own shooting.

Corry loaded his gun again, and on they went; but pretty soon he remarked, —

"We're in the swamp now, Port."

"I don't see any swamp: it's all trees and bushes and snow."

"That's so, but there's ice under the snow in some places. You can't get through here at all in the spring, and hardly in summer. It's a great place for rabbits."

Ponto was doubtless aware of that fact, for he was dashing to and fro most industriously.

There were plenty of little tracks on the snow, as the boys could now plainly see; but they crossed each other in all directions, after a manner that puzzled Porter Hudson exceedingly.

"How will he find out which one of them he'd better follow up?"

"Wait, Port: you'll see."

Porter was taking his first lesson as a sportsman, and was peering anxiously behind trees and in among the nearest bushes. Suddenly he saw something, or thought he saw it, which made him hold his breath and tremblingly lift his gun.

"Can that be a real rabbit," he thought, "sitting there so still?"

He did not utter a loud word; and the first Corry heard about it was from both barrels of his cousin's gun, fired in quick succession. Bang, bang! they went.

"What is it, Port?"

"I've got him! I've got him!"

He was bounding away across the snow, and disappeared among some thick hazel-bushes. A moment more, and he was out again, with a rabbit in his hand every ounce as big as the one Corry had killed.

"First-rate, Port! Was he running?"

"No, he was sitting still, and listening for something."

Corry was too polite to say that no regular sportsman fired at a rabbit unless it was running. It would have been a pity to have dampened Porter Hudson's tremulous exultation over his first game.

He held that rabbit up, and looked at it, until he grew red in the face.

He had no time to talk then; for he had his gun to load, and he was in no small anxiety as to whether he should succeed in getting the charge in rightly. Besides, there was Ponto racing across the farther side of the swamp, with a big rabbit just ahead of him. He was a capital jumper, that rabbit, and he was gaining on his barking pursuer when he ran out within range of Corry Farnham's gun.

Only one barrel was fired, but Ponto's master was ahead again.

"Two to my one," said Porter.

"You'll have chances enough. Don't you let off both barrels every time, though, or you may lose some of 'em. Fill your rabbits all full of shot, too, like that one."

Port's idea had been that both barrels of his gun were there for the purpose of being fired off, but he was quite ready to take a hint. He had more and more serious doubts, however, about his ability to hit a rabbit on the run. The first time he actually tried to do it, he doubted more than ever. His chance and his disappointment came to him a little after Corry's gun was loaded, and while they were crossing the swamp.

"I must have hit him," he said, as he lowered his gun, and looked after the rabbit he had fired at, and which was still clearing the snow with long, vigorous jumps.

"Well, if you did," said Corry, "he hasn't found it out yet."

"Your first one didn't find out he was hit till he got into the tree."

"That's so. But I never knew it to happen just so before. Ponto's after that one again! He's turned him around those sumach-bushes. He's coming this way. Give him your other barrel. Shoot ahead of him."

Porter was positive, in his own mind, that he could not hit that rabbit, and he felt himself blushing as he raised his gun; but he tried to see the rabbit somewhere beyond the end of it, and then he blazed away.

"I declare! you've done it! A good long distance too."

It was so very long, that the shot had scattered a great deal, and one of the little leaden pellets had strayed in the direction of that rabbit, — just one, but it was as good as a dozen, for it had struck in a vital spot; and Porter was as proud as if the skin of his game had been filled with shot-holes.

"I'm even with you now."

"That's so. If you only had practice, you'd shoot well enough."

Almost two hours went by, after that, and they tramped all over the swamp. Porter killed another sitting rabbit; but Corry was again one ahead of him, and was feeling half sorry for it, when he suddenly stopped marching, and lifted his hand, exclaiming, —

"Hear Ponto! Hark! Away yonder!"

"Started another rabbit."

"No, he hasn't. It isn't any rabbit this time."

"What is it? What is it?"

"Hear that jumping? Hear Ponto's yelp? It's a deer."

"Deer! Did you say it was a deer? Can you tell?"

"Hark! Listen!"

Ponto was no deer-hound. He was somewhat too heavily built for that kind of sport; but any deer of good common sense would get away from his neighborhood, all the same. The certainty that the dog could not catch him would not interfere with his running.

Ponto's discovery was a really splendid buck, and he was in a terrible hurry when his long, easy bounds brought him out from among the forest-trees into the more open ground in the edge of the swamp. Porter thought he had never before seen any thing half so exciting, but the buck went by like a flash.

Just half a minute later, Corry turned ruefully to his cousin, and asked him, —

"Port, what did you and I fire both barrels of our guns for?"

"Why, to hit the deer."

"At that distance? And with small shot too? If they'd reached him, they'd hardly have stung him. Let's go home."

Porter was ready enough; and it was not long before even Ponto gave up following the buck, and came panting along at the heels of his master. He looked a little crestfallen, as if he were nearly prepared to remark, —

"No use to drive deer for boys. I did my duty. No dog of my size and weight can do more."

They had a tramp before them. Not that they were so far from home, but then it was one long wade through the snow until they reached the road; and Porter Hudson knew much more about the weight of rabbits by the time he laid his game down at the kitchen-door of the farmhouse.

They had been growing heavier and heavier all the way, until he almost wished he had not killed more than one.

CHAPTER IV.

WINTER COMFORT.

Susie and Pen had a grand ride to the farmhouse
on the wood-sleigh.

Perched away up there on top of the brushwood,
they could get the full effect of every swing and
lurch of the load under them. Vosh Stebbins had
to chuckle again and again, in spite of his resolute
politeness; for the girls would scream a little, and
laugh a great deal, when the sleigh sank suddenly on
one side in a snowy hollow, or slid too rapidly after
the oxen down a steeper slope than common. It
was great fun; and, when they reached the house,
Susie Hudson almost had to quarrel with aunt Judith
to prevent being wrapped in a blanket, and shoved
up in a big rocking-chair into the very face of the
sitting-room fireplace.

"Do let her alone, Judith," said aunt Farnham.
"I don't believe she's been frost-bitten."

"I'm not a bit cold."

"I'm real glad o' that," said aunt Judith; "but ain't you hungry? — Pen, you jest fetch up some krullers."

Susie admitted that she could eat a kruller, and Pen had no need to be told twice.

When Vosh came back from the woods with his second load, it was dinner-time; and Deacon Farnham came with him. Only a few minutes later, there was a great shouting at the kitchen-door, and there were the two boys. The whole family rushed out to see what they had brought home, and Susie thought she had never seen her brother look quite so tall.

"Corry beat ye, did he?" said Vosh as he turned the rabbits over. Something in the tone of that remark seemed to add, "Of course he did;" and Port replied to it, —

"Well, he's used to it. I never fired a gun before in all my life."

That was a frank confession, and a very good one to make; for the deacon exclaimed, —

"You never did! I declare! then you've done tip-top. You'll make a marksman one of these days."

"I hit two of my rabbits on the full run, anyhow."

"How about the deer?" said Vosh with a sly look. "Did you hit him on the run?"

"When you meet him," said Corry, "you can

just ask him. He's the only fellow that knows: I don't."

"Like as not he doesn't either."

"Vosh," said Mrs. Farnham, "tell your mother to come over with you after tea, and spend the evening."

"She'll come: I know she will. I'll finish my chores early."

He swung his axe to his shoulder, and marched away, very straight, with a curious feeling that some city people were looking at him.

The boys and the girls and the older people were all remarkably ready for that dinner as soon as it was on the table.

"Pen," said Susie, "I didn't know chopping down trees would make me so hungry."

"Yes," said Deacon Farnham, "it's as bad as killing deer. Port and Corry are suffering from that. You did your chopping, as they did their deer-killing, at a safe distance."

After dinner it was a puzzle to everybody where the time went, it got away so fast. Pen took Susie all over the house, and showed her every thing in it, from the apples in the cellar to the spinning-wheel that had been carried up stairs the day before, and would have to come down again to-morrow.

"Aunt Judith's got a pile of wool, Susie. You ought to see it. She's going to spin enough yarn to last her all next summer."

"I'll get her to teach me to spin."

"Can you knit? If you can't, I'll teach you how. It's awful easy, as soon as you know."

Susie told Pen about her tidies and crochet-work and some other things, and was getting a little the best of it, until Pen asked very doubtfully, —

"Can you heel a stocking? It's worse, a good deal, than just to narrow 'em in at the toes. Aunt Judith says there ain't many women nowadays that can heel a stocking."

"I'll make her show me how. Dear me, Pen! did you know how late it is? Where can all the time have gone to?"

Corry and Porter knew where a part of theirs had gone, after they got back from the barns, and delivered to Mrs. Farnham and aunt Judith the eggs they had found. Corry got out his checker-board, and laid it on the table in the sitting-room.

"It's a big one," said Porter. "Where are your men?"

"Hanging up there in that bag. The wooden men got lost. We take horse-chestnuts for black men, and walnuts for white ones."

"S'pose you make a king?"

"That's a butternut, if it's black. If it's white, you put on one of those chunks of wood."

There was no danger of their getting out of checker-men; but Corry Farnham had a lesson to learn.

Porter Hudson knew a great deal more about checkers than he did about tree-chopping or rabbits.

Game after game was played, and it seemed to Corry as if his cousin "hit some of them on a full run." He got up from the last one they played, feeling a very fair degree of respect for Port; and the latter was pretty well restored to his own good opinion of himself.

That was something, for all his morning's experiences had been a little the other way; and he was not half sure he could again hit a running rabbit, if he should have a chance to try.

Susie and Pen had watched them for a while, but both boys had been very obstinate in not making any of the good moves Pen pointed out to them.

There were chores to do both before and after tea; and Porter went out with Corry, determined on undertaking his share of them.

"Did you ever milk cows, Port?"

"Well, no, I never did; but I guess I could if I tried."

"Well, I guess you'd best not try to-night, but you can learn before you go home. Some of our cows are skittish in cold weather."

Port was quite contented, after getting into the cowyard, to let the milking be done by some one who knew how; and he had the satisfaction of seeing Corry kicked over into the snow — pail, milk, and all

— by a brindled heifer who had no need of any kind of weather to bring out her natural skittishness.

There were pigs and cattle and horses to feed, and supper to be eaten; and when, at last, the boys had finished their duties, the rest of the family was already gathered in the sitting-room.

Mrs. Farnham and aunt Judith had their knitting; and the deacon had a newspaper in his lap, with his spectacles lying in the middle of it. It seemed, however, the most natural thing in the world, that they should all be sitting in a great semicircle in front of the fireplace. The night promised to be a cold one, and the fire had been built for it in the most liberal manner.

"Corry," said Porter, "what are all those flat-irons and hammers for?"

"Why, to crack nuts. I'm going down cellar to bring 'em up, — butternuts and hickory-nuts. There was a big crop of 'em last fall."

"I'll go with you."

"So will I," said Pen. "Come, Susie, and we'll bring up the apples and pears and some cider."

"Now, Pen," said aunt Judith, "look out you don't leave the cider runnin', like you did once. You may fetch up a cake of maple-sugar, if anybody wants any. And don't you tetch them hard russets. They won't be fit to eat till spring."

Aunt Judith's instructions continued almost without cessation, till the young folk were all at the bottom of the cellar-stairs. Corry and Pen carried candles; but the light of these only served to make that cellar look ten times larger and darker and more mysterious. It seemed as if it had neither sides nor ends; but the heavy black beams overhead were not so wonderfully far away. Pen showed Susie bin after bin of carefully selected winter apples and pears, and there were half a dozen barrels of cider ranged against the wall.

"It's all pretty sweet now, but it'll be hard enough some time. Then some of it'll make vinegar."

"What's in the little barrel?"

"Aunt Judith's currant-wine. She says it'll be the best wine in the world when it's old enough. Whenever anybody in the Valley gets sick, she takes a bottle of it, and goes there."

"She's real good."

"Susie, look at all the mince-pies on the swing-shelf."

"Ever so many!"

Scores of them, for the swing-shelf ran the whole length of the cellar right down the middle, and it held double rows of pies all ready to be carried up and warmed for use. Susie would have been willing to stay a few minutes, and look at the treasures in that cellar; but Corry suddenly exclaimed, —

"Port, let's hurry. They've come. Don't you hear Mrs. Stebbins?"

Just a little before that, aunt Judith up stairs had turned to the deacon with the remark, —

"Joshaway, I knew she'd come with Vosh. You can always hear her before she gets to the gate; leastwise, on a quiet night like this. I remember one night it was a-stormin', and the wind blew so hard she got right up to the door, and I hadn't heard a sound till she had her hand on the latch."

They could hear her now.

"And, Lavawjer, you must just mind one thing: you mustn't talk too much. Let them do their own talkin', specially Susie. I can't begin to tell what kind of a gal she's growin' up to be, onless I can hear her talk."

"Then Vosh'll have to keep a-givin' his mother somethin' to eat," snapped aunt Judith: "she never stops talkin' any other time."

Mrs. Farnham herself, while the young people were down stairs, had thoughtfully walked out into the storeroom adjoining the kitchen, and returned with a long-handled wire corn-popper, and a bag of what she called "'tucket corn." It was corn with small, round, blue-black kernels, that can pop out larger and whiter, for its size, than any other kind that grows. There is a legend that the seed of it came originally from the island of Nantucket; but it has short "nubbin" ears, and even the island Indians must have found it a poor crop for any thing but popping.

Mrs. Stebbins was at the door now; and she never dreamed of knocking, and waiting out there in the cold until somebody should come to let her in. She was hardly over the threshold, before she said, as she loosened her shawl, —

"Judith, where is Susie and her brother, and Corry and Pen? They haven't gone away somewhere the very first night, have they? Vosh he told me they'd be at home, and I just thought I'd come over."

"They're down cellar. They'll be right up in a minute. Now, Angeline, you jest take off your hood and sit down. — Vosh, there's a chair. Hadn't you better take that popper and set to work?"

"Vosh tells me," continued his mother, "the boys got half a dozen of rabbits to-day. I don't care much for rabbits, but their hind-legs'll do to brile. And they seen a deer too. I'd ha' thought they might ha' shot it, if it was nigh enough. But then, deer isn't anyways like as easy to kill as they was when I was a gal. And they was only a couple of boys. I do say, now, here they come, and they're makin' racket enough for twenty."

They were coming indeed, streaming up out of the cellar, with every pair of hands full and a little more; and Mrs. Stebbins did not stop for an instant.

"Susie, is that you? Well, now, I must kiss you right away. Vosh said you was lookin' real pretty,

and so you be ; but he ain't always a good jedge. I
knowed your mother when she wasn't no older'n
you be now. She was Joshaway Farnham's sister.
And so she's gone South for her health, and your
father's gone with her, and you've come to put in
the rest of your winter up here? — I do declare, Lavawjer, ef you ain't kerful, you'll burn up every ker-
nel of that corn. Don't you stop to talk, and gawk
around. Jest you tend to your corn-poppin'."

She had managed to get up from her chair and
kiss Susie without interrupting the steady clack of
her tongue ; but she was a little out of breath for a
moment, and sat still and watched them while they
deposited upon the table the tall brown pitcher of
cider, the pans of fruit, and the maple-sugar. The
young folks had a chance to say a word to Vosh,
and Corry and Porter each picked up a flat-iron and
a hammer. There were plenty of nuts ready for
them ; and the sound of the cracking, and of the
rattling, bursting corn in the popper, mingled oddly
with Susie's efforts to answer the rapid inquiries
poured upon her by Mrs. Stebbins.

"Now, Susie, I'm glad you've come. You're right
from the city, and you're a well-grown gal now, and
you know all about the fashions. We don't hear a
word about 'em up here away till they've all come
and gone, and somethin' else is in fashion. Got to
wearin' short dresses, hev they? Think of me, or

Judith, or your aunt Sarah Farnham, in short dresses! Wearin' panners too. I do say! What won't they put on next! Last thing they got up was them little skimp skirts for hard times, that came so nigh bein' the ruin of the dry-goods men. Didn't take no cloth at all. — Lavawjer, you're a-talkin' again. You just tend to your pop-corn."

"Now, Angeline," said Mrs. Farnham, "do take an apple, or a pear."

"Yes, Angeline," said aunt Judith, "and here's a plate of popped corn, and some nuts. — Joshaway, pour her out a mug of cider. — Pen, go to the cupboard and fetch a plate of krullers. It's the coldest kind of a night."

"So it is," began Mrs. Stebbins, "but the winters ain't what they used to be. No more the butternuts aren't, somehow; but I must say, you make out to have good fruit, though how you do it in these times beats me. Our trees die out."

Likely as not they did; but the attack had fairly begun, and poor Mrs. Stebbins found herself outnumbered. The deacon pressed her with the cider, and Mrs. Farnham with the krullers. There was the heaped-up plate of snowy white popped corn, and beside it was the tempting little hill of cracked hickory-nuts and butternuts. Susie broke off for her a noble piece of maple-sugar; and aunt Judith herself took a candle, and went down cellar for a

couple of the best mince-pies. It was all too much
for conversation of the kind Mrs Stebbins delighted
in.

"O Vosh!" suddenly exclaimed Susie. "Corry
told us this morning about the bear you killed last
winter."

It was cruel to mention such a thing just as Mrs.
Stebbins had lifted a kruller, and she began to say, —

"Yes, about that bear. Lavawjer's father"— But
she had to pause a moment, and Vosh took it up
with, —

"No, Susie, I didn't kill him : I guess it was all
three of us. He was chockfull of lead when he rolled
over. We weren't twenty feet from him. Deacon
Farnham he fired first, and then I did, and Corry ;
and we all had double-barrelled guns, and we didn't
one of us miss. But it was a big bear"—

"Biggest kind," said Corry, "or he never could
ha' lifted a fat hog clean out of the pen the way he
did."

"I knowed a bear," began Mrs. Stebbins ; but
aunt Judith interrupted her with, —

"Now, Angeline, do take a slice of mince-pie.
It's cold, but sometimes it's better cold than it is
when it's warm."

The pie was too much for the memory of that
other bear.

The sound of popping corn and cracking nuts had

been almost incessant, and the young people had now succeeded in breaking all the ice the fire had left in that sitting-room. They were old acquaintances all around, and were chatting away merrily among themselves, with less and less reference to what might be going forward among the old folk by the table.

Mrs. Farnham and aunt Judith seemed to keep right along with their knitting, whatever else they might be doing. It seemed to do itself, a great deal like their breathing. Even the deacon managed to look into the corners of his newspaper while he pared an apple, or talked to Mrs. Stebbins. The light of the great astral-lamp on the table mingled with that from the fireplace in a sort of reddish-golden glow, that flickered over the walls and faces in a way to make every thing and every body wear a warm, contented, cosey look, that was just the right thing for a frosty winter evening.

By and by there came almost a full half-minute of silence, and at the end of it Vosh burst out as if an idea had taken him by surprise.

"I do declare! I never saw any thing jollier'n this is, in all my born days."

"Vosh," said Corry, "Port can beat you at checkers. You ought to have seen the way he beat me to-day. You just try him a game."

"Now, Lavawjer," said his mother from beyond

the table, "you kin play well enough for way up here, but you can't think of comin' up to sech a young feller as Porter Hudson. He'll beat ye, sure."

At all events, he needed no more than that to make him try to do it; and Penelope brought out the great square board, and the bag of home-made checkers.

It must be confessed, that, after his triumphant experience with Corry, Porter Hudson imagined himself to have quite taken the measure of up-country skill and science at that game. He sat down to his new trial, therefore, with a proud assurance of a victory to come. It would have been kind of Corry to have given his cousin the least bit of a warning, but that young gentleman had been himself too roughly handled to feel very merciful. Besides, he had some very small and lingering doubt as to the result, and was willing to wait for it.

He need not have had any doubt, since there was really no room for any. Vosh was a born checker-player, and it is never easy to beat a fellow of that sort. Nobody ever knows exactly how they do it, and they themselves cannot tell. Their spare men get to the king-row, and their calculations come out right; and if you are Porter Hudson, and are playing against them, you get beaten very badly, and there's no help for you.

Corry watched that game with a suppressed chuckle, but it was a dreadful puzzle to Port. Even

Pen did not venture to suggest a single good move, and the older people talked very quietly.

Mrs. Stebbins was a proud woman when Susie exclaimed, —

"Vosh has won it!"

It was of no use for aunt Judith to say, —

"Won't you have another slice of pie, Angeline, and some more cider?"

Mrs. Stebbins responded, —

"I don't keer if I do. Only I'm afeard it'll make me dream and talk in my sleep. Lavawjer always did play checkers mighty spry, but he ain't the player his father was when he was a young man. He didn't have no time to play checkers after he got to runnin' a farm of his own. Pie? Yes, Judith, you've got jest the right knack of makin' mince-pies." And while she went on to tell of the various good and bad pies she had seen or tasted, all the rest agreed with her about those they were eating. In fact, the good things of all sorts went far to reconcile even Porter Hudson to his defeat, and Vosh was truly polite about that. In less than two minutes he managed to get the other boys, and even the girls, talking about hunting, skating, coasting, sleigh-riding, and catching fish through the ice.

The evening seemed to melt away, it went so fast; and no one was willing to believe how late it was when Mrs. Stebbins began to put on her hood. They all saw her and Vosh to the door, and did not close that until the gate shut behind the last words the good woman succeeded in sending back to them.

It was something about boiled cider in mince-pies, but they failed to get it.

CHAPTER V.

A WINTER PICNIC-PARTY.

The Stebbins farm was not a large one, and neither its house nor barns compared well with Deacon Farnham's; but there was a great deal to be done in and around them, even in winter. Vosh was a busy boy, therefore, the next morning, and his mother was a busy woman; and it was not until an hour after breakfast that she said to him, —

"Now, Lavawjer, you jest hitch up that there new red cutter of yourn, and fetch it around. I want you to drive me to Benton Village, and, if I can't find what I want there, I'm goin' right on to Cobbleville."

Vosh had been thinking up a series of excuses for going over to the deacon's, but he made no mention of them; and it was a credit to him that his new turnout was so soon standing, all ready, by the front gate.

It was not a bad idea, that his first long drive in

65

it should be with his mother; but he had a string of surprises before him that day.

The first came in the fact that his mother was unaccountably silent, and that, whenever she did open her lips, she had something to say about economy. Then she talked a little of the wickedness and vanity of buying or wearing any thing "just for show." City people, she freely declared, were doing that very thing all the while, and she was glad enough no one alive could accuse her of it.

Vosh was quite sure she was right; but he could not help, when they drove by Deacon Farnham's, and he saw the girls at the window, being a little glad that his cutter was of so bright a red, and so remarkably well varnished.

Benton Village was right down there in the valley, and the sorrel colt pulled them there in so short a time that it was no sleigh-ride at all.

Mrs. Stebbins said as much, after she had bought some tea and sugar at one store, and some raisins and some coffee at another.

"They haven't got what I want, Lavawjer. You kin drive right along to Cobbleville. There never was better sleighin', not even when I was a gal."

That was a great deal for her to admit, and Vosh put the colt to his very best speed along the well-travelled road to Cobbleville. That was several long miles, but they were strangely silent ones.

"Where shall I pull up, mother?" asked Vosh as they drove into the one long street of the village.

"You kin make your first stop right there, at old Gillis's harness-shop. I want to look at some o' them things in his front winder."

Something or other must have winked at Vosh; for he was out of that cutter, and had his colt hitched in front of Gillis's, in about half his usual time.

"Lavawjer," she said to him as she paused on the sidewalk, "don't you ever buy a thing just for show. You mustn't ever let your vanity get the best of you."

Two minutes later she was holding in her right hand a very useful string of sleigh-bells, and saying to him, —

"Now, Lavawjer, if you're ever drivin' along after dark, you won't be run into. Anybody'll know you're there, by the jingle. I'll kinder feel safer about ye."

Vosh thought he had not often seen less vanity in any thing than there was in those bells, and he was thinking of going right out to put them on the sorrel, when his mother exclaimed, —

"There! that's what I've been a-lookin' for, — that there red hoss-blanket, with the blue border and the fringe. Jest tell me what the price of it is."

It was only a very little, the best blanket in the shop; and she said to her son, —

"I don't know but it's kinder showy. You can't

exactly help that. But it won't do for you to let that colt of yourn git warm, drivin' him sharp, and then let him catch cold when you hitch him. You must take keer of him, and see't he has his blanket on. You'll find it mighty useful."

"Guess I will!" said Vosh, with a queer feeling that he ought to say something grateful, and didn't know how. He was thinking about it, when his mother said to him, —

"That there headstall of yourn is gettin' cracked, and the check-rein might break some day. The rest of your harness'll do for a while. It's always safe to have your leather in good condition."

No doubt; and the sorrel colt was a different-looking animal when Vosh exchanged the head-gear he had worn coming, for the new rig the careful Mrs. Stebbins bought for him.

"Now, Vosh, there isn't any thing else I want in Cobbleville, but you may drive through the main street, and we'll take a look at the town."

He unhitched the colt, and sprang in after her. The new headstall, check-rein, and the bells were already in their places. The brilliant blanket was spread across their laps as they sat in the cutter. Vosh touched up the sorrel, and all the Cobbleville people who saw that turnout dash up the street for half a mile and back again were compelled to admit that it was decidedly a neat one.

"Now, Lavawjer," said his mother, "don't you never do nothin' jest for show. If you want to take Judith Farnham or her sister, or Penelope, or Susie Hudson, out a-sleighin', they won't need to turn up their noses at the rig you come after 'em in."

They had all been talking of Vosh and his mother that morning at Deacon Farnham's, and it was plain that the good qualities of the Stebbins family were fully understood by their next-door neighbors. The boys hoped Vosh would come over in the course of the day, but he did not. The next day was Saturday, and still he did not come. He was at work in his own barn, shelling corn for dear life, to let his mother know how fully he appreciated her generosity. He felt that it would take an immense deal of hard work to express all he felt about the bells and the blanket, not to speak of the bright bits of new harness.

The next day was Sunday, and Deacon Farnham's entire household went to meeting down at Benton Village. Almost all they saw of Vosh was when they turned around to look at the choir. Susie only did that once, for she somehow connected her catching his eye with the fact that he just then started on the wrong stanza of the hymn they were singing, and so got himself looked at by the choir-leader.

The next day, just after tea, Vosh came over "to have a word with Deacon Farnham," and he had an errand of some importance this time. Corry and

Porter stood by, with their mouths wide open, while he delivered it. He was just inside the kitchen-door; and Susie and Pen were sitting on the other side of the stove, paring apples.

"There was a man came by to-day from one of the lumber camps way up among the mountains. He was on his way to town for supplies and things. He says the road to Mink Lake's good enough for a sleigh."

"All the way?" asked the deacon somewhat doubtfully.

"Every inch of it: I asked him. Now, why couldn't we go in for a mess of pickerel?"

"And a grand sleigh-ride!" exclaimed Corry.

"And an old-fashioned winter picnic!" added aunt Sarah Farnham. "How would you like that, Susie?"

"A winter picnic! I never heard of such a thing. How do you do it? Seems to me it would be splendid, if you could."

"A picnic, a picnic!" shouted Pen. "Fishing through the ice, Susie, and — and — there's ever so many other things. — Mother, can we go?"

Vosh Stebbins had spoken only about the pickerel, but the larger enterprise was what had really been upon his mind. Before he went home it had been thoroughly discussed, and pretty well arranged for.

"Corry," said Port after Vosh went away, "what sort of a place is Mink Lake?"

"It's the prettiest kind of a lake. It's a great place to go to in summer, — just crowded with fish."

"Is it far?"

"About eight or nine miles, right through the woods and around among the mountains. Crookedest road you ever saw. It's apt to be snowed up in winter; but we haven't had any deep snow yet, and it hasn't drifted much, somehow."

"What kind of fish, — trout?"

"Yes, there's trout, but there's more bass and pickerel and perch. You're apt to be awfully bothered with pumpkin-seeds in summer."

Port was silent. He wanted to ask about the pumpkins, and how the seeds could bother a fellow when he was fishing for trout. After a minute or so, he uttered one word, —

"Pumpkin-seeds?"

"Crowds of 'em. They're the meanest kind of fish. Bite, bite, bite, and you keep pulling 'em in, all the while you want something bigger."

"Can't you eat 'em?"

"Yes, they're good to fry, but they're full of bones. Not enough of 'em."

"They won't bite in winter, will they?"

"Hope not. Tell you what, Port, we're in for the biggest kind of a time."

That was an exciting evening. Nobody seemed to want to go to bed, and the semicircle around the

fireplace talked of hardly any thing else but fishing
and hunting. Deacon Farnham himself came out
with some stories aunt Judith said she hadn't heard
him tell for more than a year. Porter and Susie had
no stories to tell, but they could listen. The former
went to bed at last, with a vague feeling that he
would rather go to Mink Lake. It was a good while
before he got to sleep, and even then he had a wonderful dream. He dreamed he was trying to pull a
fish as large as a small whale through a sort of
auger-hole in some ice. He pulled so hard, he woke
himself up; but he could roll over and go to sleep
soundly, now the fish was gone.

The house was early astir in the morning; and
Deacon Farnham's long, low box-sleigh, drawn by
his two big black horses, was at the door by the
time they were through breakfast. Mrs. Farnham
had decided not to go, because, as she said, —

"It's Judith's turn. Somebody's got to stay and
keep house."

It had required some argument to persuade aunt
Judith that it was her duty to go, but she had taken
hold of the preparations with a will. It was wonderful what an amount of wrapping-up she deemed necessary for herself and all the rest.

"Why, Judith," said the deacon, "it's a good deal
warmer in the woods than it is out here."

"I've heerd tell so, and mebbe it's true, but I

don't put any trust in it. I've no notion of bein' frost-bit before I get back."

There was little to be feared from the frost, with all the buffalo-robes and blankets and shawls and cloaks that were piled into that sleigh. .

When its passengers were in, they made quite a party. There was the deacon (who insisted on driving), and aunt Judith, and Mrs. Stebbins and Vosh, and Corry, and Susie Hudson and Porter, and Penelope, in the sleigh, with Ponto all around outside of it; besides all the baskets of luncheon, the fishing-tackle, axes, and guns.

"You can't shoot fish," said Susie.

"May shoot something else," said Vosh. "There's no such thing as telling. It's a wild place."

"Susie!" exclaimed Pen, "didn't you know there were deer up at Mink Lake,—real deer?"

"Corry," whispered Port, "let's get one before we come home."

"Father's got his gun by him, all ready, but he won't let us get ours out till we reach the lake. He may get a shot at something as he drives along."

There was a sharp lookout for all kinds of wild animals, after the way began to wind among the piny woods, and through the desolate-looking "clearings" left by the choppers. The road was found even better than Vosh's news had reported it, and the black team pulled their merry load along quite easily.

The young folk soon got over the solemn feeling which came upon them when they found themselves actually in the great forest.

It was delightful to shout, and listen for echoes; and to sing, and know there was not a living pair of ears to hear, except those in the sleigh, and Ponto's.

It was about two hours after they left the farm-house, and Port had just remarked, —

"Seems to me we've been going up hill all the time," when Corry suddenly exclaimed, —

"There it is! That's Mink Lake. It'll be down hill all the way going home. See it!"

"Lake!" said Port. "I don't see any lake. Oh, yes, I do! It's all ice and snow, — frozen clean over."

"And we haven't seen a single deer yet," said Susie sorrowfully.

"You can see some now, then," replied Vosh as he eagerly pointed forward. "See 'em, Susie? See 'em? Way down yonder on the ice."

"I see them!" shouted Pen. "One, two, three, *four* of 'em."

"Those black specks?" said Susie.

There they were indeed, and they were beginning to move rapidly across the ice; but they were too far away for any thing more than just to make out what they were.

Even Ponto continued to plod along soberly be-hind the sleigh. He was too old a dog to excite himself over any such distant and impossible game as that.

Deacon Farnham seemed to know exactly what he was about; for he drove right on where nobody else could see any road, until he stopped in front of a very small and very rudely made kind of house.

"Aunt Judith," asked Susie, "did anybody ever live here?"

"Live here, child? Why, that there's a choppers' shanty. It's for anybody that wants it, now they've done with it."

That was so, but it was not for the mere human beings of that picnic-party. The deacon took his horses from the sleigh, and led them in through the rickety door.

"They're a little warm," he said, "but they won't catch cold in there. I'll give 'em a good feed, Vosh, while you're starting a fire. — Get the guns and tackle out, Corry."

Vosh had had a hard struggle with himself that morning to leave his own horse and cutter at home; but his mother had settled it for him. She remarked, —

"I'd ruther be in the big sleigh with the folks, so I can hear what's goin' on. So would Susie Hudson, or aunt Judith Farnham. You'd be kind o' lonely. Besides, that little thing of yourn 'd be upsettin' twenty times, over them mountain roads."

He was ready with his axe now; and Porter Hudson opened his eyes at the rapidity with which a great fire was blazing on the snow, a little distance from the shanty.

"What are we to get into?" asked Port.

"We won't need any shelter," said aunt Judith. "When it's time for dinner, we can eat it in the sleigh."

They were not yet thinking of eating. The first business on hand was a trip to the lake. Vosh Stebbins took his axe with him, and he and the deacon each carried a long, wide board. Port managed not to ask what these were for, and he had not a great while to wait before he knew.

"Vosh," said the deacon, "the ice must be pretty thick. Hope we sha'n't have to chop a hole."

"There's one air-hole, away yonder. It doesn't look too wide."

"Shouldn't wonder if it'd do."

"Susie," said Pen, "don't you know? That's where all the fish come up to the top to get a breath of fresh air."

There was some truth in Pen's explanation, in spite of the laugh she got from Mrs. Stebbins. Susie said nothing, for she was all eyes at that moment. She thought she had never seen any thing stranger or more beautiful than that little lake, all frozen, with the hills around it, and the mountains beyond them. The broken slopes of the hills and mountains were covered with white snow, green pines, spruces, hemlocks, and with the brownish gray of the other trees whose leaves had fallen from them. It was very wonderful and new to a young lady from the city.

"Most half the lake," said Vosh, "is smooth enough to skate on. If I'd ha' thought of that, I'd ha' brought along my skates."

It would have been worth while. Mink Lake was what some people call a "pond," and was hardly a mile wide by an irregular mile and a half long. There was an immense skating-rink there now, in spite of the snow which covered a large part of it.

Susie was just about to ask some more questions, when her uncle shouted, —

"This'll do, Vosh! Bring along your slide."

That was the board he was carrying, and its use was plain now. The air-hole was an opening in the ice, not more than two feet across, but the ice was thin at the edges of it. A heavy man, or a busy one, might break through, and let himself into a cold bath; but when those two "slides" were slipped along on either side of the hole, any one could walk right out, and drop in a hook and line safely enough.

"There, Susie," said Pen, "now we can keep our feet dry while we catch our fish."

"Now, folks!" exclaimed the deacon. "Two at a time. We'll take turns."

"Your turn's good till you've hooked a fish," said Vosh to Porter, as he handed him a line. "You and the deacon try it first."

It seemed very easy, — nothing to do but to stand on a dry board, and drop a line with a baited hook at the end of it through a two-foot hole in the ice. There was no long waiting to be done either.

"Father, father!" shouted Pen in a few moments. "You've got him!" There was a sort of electric shock went through the entire picnic; but the deacon jerked out a very good-looking fish with an unthankful look on his face.

"Nothing but a perch. He's a pound and a quarter, though. — Here, Mrs. Stebbins, take that other line, and see what you can do."

Mrs. Stebbins had talked quite industriously all the way, and even after they got upon the ice; but she stopped short the moment she took hold of that line. She had hardly dropped it in, before Porter Hudson exclaimed, —

"Corry, Corry!"

"Pull, Port! Pull! You've got a big one."

"So have I," screamed Mrs. Stebbins. "Deacon! — Vosh! It's awful! Come help me!"

"Pen," said Susie, "could it pull her through the hole?"

"Why, Susie!"

Pen's eyes and mouth were wide open; for both

her cousin and Mrs. Stebbins were leaning back, and it seemed as if something down below were jerking at them.

"Wind it round your wrist, Port," said Corry. "Hang on!"

"Now, mother," said Vosh as he took hold of her line, "I declare, you *have* hooked a good one. I guess I'll pull him in for you."

It hardly seemed to cost him an effort to bring a great three-pound pickerel through the hole, and sling him out upon the ice.

"That's better than perch, deacon."

"Shall I help you, Port?" asked Corry.

"No, sir-e-e-e! I'll bring in my own fish."

"Hand over hand! Don't let him get away from you."

Port's blood was up, now he had seen that other pickerel landed, and he pulled with all his might.

"Now lift," said Vosh. "Don't let him rub his nose against the ice, or he'll break loose. Don't lean over too far. That's it."

It was splendidly exciting; and Port followed the directions given him, although his heart was beating quickly, and he thought he had never lifted any thing else quite so heavy as that fish.

"Out he comes!" he shouted.

"Hurrah for Port!" said aunt Judith. "It's the biggest one yet."

So it was; and a proud boy was Porter Hudson when Deacon Farnham declared that the great fish he had fought so hard with was a seven-pound pickerel.

"Now, aunt Judith, it's your turn next."

"Me, Corry? Me? What could I do with a cretur like that?"

"I'll help you if you get a big one. Here's your line: you must try."

She had to be coaxed a little more, but she consented, and Susie herself took the other line. The fish were biting hungrily; for in less than a minute aunt Judith gave a little scream and a jerk, and began to pull in her line; then another little scream and another jerk, and then, —

"Perch!" she exclaimed. "Ain't I glad it wasn't a pickerel!—Penelope, you can ketch the rest of my fish for me. I'll just look on."

Susie's face grew almost pale, as she stood there with her line in her hand, waiting for something to pull on it.

"Do they nibble first, Vosh?"

Hardly were the words out of her mouth, before her line was suddenly jerked away from her. Vosh had just time to catch hold of the piece of wood the rest of it was wound upon.

"I've lost him, I've lost him!"

"No, you haven't, but he's running pretty well.

Guess I'd better snub him. He'd have cut your fingers with the line if you'd ha' tried."

Susie's soft white hands were hardly suited to work of that sort, and they were already getting a little cold. She was quite willing to pick up her muff, and slip them into it while Vosh pulled in her pickerel for her. It was a right good one too, only a little less weighty than Porter's.

Pen had now taken the line from aunt Judith, and she dropped her hook in very confidently.

" There isn't a scrap of bait on it," said Corry.

"Isn't there? I forgot that. Just wait a minute, and then I'll let you put some on."

Corry and the rest began to laugh, but Pen shouted again, —

"He's nibbling! Now he's biting! Oh, he's bit!"

So he had, bait or no bait; and she was quite strong enough to pull up a very handsome perch without help from anybody.

After that, Deacon Farnham and the boys had the fishing all to themselves. It was well there was enough of it to make it exciting; for it was wet, cold, chilly work. The fish were of several sorts and all sizes; and some of them rubbed themselves free against the icy edges of the hole, in spite of all that could be done. Before noon there was a consider-able pile of them lying on the ice, and the fun of catching them had lost a little of its power to keep the cold away.

Long before the fishermen decided that they had caught enough, Mrs. Stebbins and aunt Judith and the girls got tired of looking on, and set out across the ice towards the sleigh and the very attractive-looking fire. The latter had been well heaped up at first, and was now blazing vigorously.

"We must have a good dinner ready for 'em," said aunt Judith when she turned away, — "all the fish they can eat."

"You carry one," said Mrs. Stebbins: "I'll take a couple more. The girls can help. We'll brile 'em, and we'll fry 'em, and we'll roast 'em in the ashes."

She tried to think of some other way, but she could not. She and aunt Judith were excellent cooks, and knew just what to do with fresh fish and such a fire. It was by no means their first picnic either, and the right things to cook with had not been left at home. Susie and Pen entered into the spirit of it with a vast deal of enthusiasm, but they were quite contented to let the more experienced cooks clean the fish.

"We're having the splendidest kind of a time, ain't we?" said Pen.

"Splendid! It's the first winter picnic I ever heard of."

"I never had one before, but I've heard mother tell of 'em."

There was plenty to do; and when at last the fishermen gave up dropping lines through the air-hole, and came plodding slowly back across the ice, there was all the dinner they could reasonably ask for, hot and smoking, and ready for them.

Such noble strings of fish they were dragging after them, and such hearty appetites they brought to that tempting "spread"!

There was hot coffee to be drank out of tin cups, fish in several styles of cookery, crisp fried pork, roasted potatoes, bread and butter, and last of all was some cold meat that nobody seemed to care for.

"Will there be any dessert?" asked Port.

"Aunt Judith's got some mince-pies warming on the log by the fire."

"What a dinner for the woods!"

"Woods! Why, the choppers have fresh fish and potatoes and coffee all the while, and sometimes they have venison."

"Game," said Port, "but no pie."

"Vosh," said Susie, "what has become of all your deer?"

Just at that moment they heard old Ponto barking away at a great rate in the woods near by; and Vosh sprang up, exclaiming, —

"He's treed something!"

"Guess he has," said the deacon. "Get your guns, boys. Load with buckshot."

"Mine's loaded," said Vosh.

"Mine'll be ready in a minute," said Corry. "Quick now, Port!"

"Hold on," said the deacon. "We must all have a share in the fun, if there is any."

It seemed to Susie and Pen that they could hardly wait for those two guns to be loaded; and Mrs. Stebbins exclaimed, —

"Judith, I do hate a gun; but I'm a-goin' with 'em. Ain't you?"

"Course I am. Just hark to that there dog!"

He must have shared in the general impatience, to judge by the noise he was making; and now there came another and a very curious kind of sound from that direction.

"It's a baby crying," said Pen.

"Or a cat," began Port.

"Sakes alive!" exclaimed Mrs. Stebbins. "I do believe the critter's gone and treed a wildcat."

"I guess that's it," said the deacon.

It was indeed that precisely.

They all kept together, as they waded through the snow to a spot about twenty rods into the woods, from which they could see old Ponto bounding hither and thither around the trunk of a tall maple-tree that stood by itself in the middle of an open space in the forest.

"No other tree handy for him to jump into," said Vosh. "There he is!"

"Where?" asked aunt Judith.

"See him? Up there on that big lower limb!"

"It's a good forty feet from the ground," said the deacon. "Come on, boys. — All the rest stay here."

"O Pen!" said Susie, "I do believe I'm afraid. Will he jump?"

"They'll shoot him down, and then Ponto'll grab him."

"He'd make short work of one dog, if he once got at him," said Corry. "Too much for Ponto."

There was little doubt of that, for it was a wildcat of the very largest size; not so dangerous an animal as a panther, but a terribly hard scratcher, and apt to require a great deal of killing.

He seemed even larger than he really was, as he drew himself up on the long, bare limb of the tree, and looked down so savagely upon his barking enemy.

It may be that the smell of the cookery, particularly of the fish, had tempted him so near the picnic. Then Ponto had scented him in turn, and had chased him into that solitary tree.

"Now, boys," said Deacon Farnham, "all around the tree! Fire as soon as you can after I do, but keep your second barrels. We may have to give him more lead, even if we knock him down."

Porter Hudson knew he was not one bit scared, and wondered why he should shake so when he tried to lift his gun and take aim. He was sure he could not shoot straight, and hoped the shot would scatter well.

"Now, boys!" Bang! went the deacon's gun; and the other three followed, aim or no aim. The wildcat replied with an angry scream, and began to tear the bark of the limb with his sharp, strong claws. How they would have gone through any kind of flesh!

That was only for a second or so; and then he suddenly gathered himself for a spring at the spot nearly under him, where Ponto was furiously barking.

Alas for the great cat of the woods! Too many buckshot had struck him, and he fell short of his mark in the snow.

Vosh had been watching, and he was nearest. Hardly did the wounded animal reach the snow, before Susie saw Vosh spring forward, and fire the second barrel of his gun.

"He's a real brave fellow."

"So he is," said Pen and aunt Judith; but Mrs. Stebbins was too proud of her boy to say a word.

That was very nearly enough. Corry ran forward, and Porter after him, and the deacon followed; but Ponto was ahead of them all, and it would not do to fire at any risk of shooting the brave old dog.

There was no fight left in the wildcat when Ponto's teeth were buried in his neck; and he therefore had all the fun and glory of a great shaking and growling and worrying, without any danger of being scratched.

"Drop him, Ponto, drop him!" said the deacon. "I don't want that skin spoiled: it's a fine one. We didn't put as many shot into him as I thought we would."

He was killed now, surely enough, however, and Vosh could carry him to the sleigh; and they could all go back, and eat more pie, and talk about bears and wolves and panthers, till the two girls felt like looking around at the woods to see if any of that sort of people were coming.

"We don't need any more fish," said aunt Judith: "we've more'n enough for the whole neighborhood."

"No, we don't," said the deacon. "What's more, it looks some like a snow-storm. We'd best be packing up for home."

Even that was grand fun; but it seemed almost a pity to leave so good a fire behind them to burn itself out all alone there in the snow, with nobody to sit around it, and cook, and tell stories.

"It's a waste of wood," remarked aunt Judith regretfully.

If the road had been "all up hill" coming to the lake, it was just as much all down hill going home again; and that sleigh-ride was about as good as any other part of the picnic.

They all thought so until they reached the farmhouse, and found what a splendid supper Mrs. Farnham had prepared for them. It was very nearly a wonder to all of them, afterwards, how it was possible they should have been so very ravenously hungry twice in the selfsame day.

"I guess it's the picnic," said Pen.

"No," said Corry, "that wouldn't be enough: it's the wildcat."

Deacon Farnham and the boys spent a great deal of time that evening over the skin of the wildcat. There was some talk of having it stuffed; but, on mature deliberation, that idea was given up. One reason was that nobody in that neighborhood knew how. Aunt Judith doubted if that fine specimen of wild fur would ever be of any mortal use, but Susie came to the rescue with an old new idea.

"Why, aunt Judith," she said, "when it's all finished, there can be a fringe put on all around, and some strong canvas on the under side, and it would make a lamp-mat for a centre-table. I saw one once."

"In the city too? What won't they do next! And I suppose they paid a high price for it. — Joshaway, you cure the skin, and Sarah and I'll make a table-rug of it."

Fresh fish will keep a long time in cold weather, and a good part of the day's finny harvest was packed away for home consumption in both houses. Still, after supper, and tired as he was, poor Vosh had to pay one penalty of so much good luck. He had to hitch up the sorrel, and drive to the houses of half a dozen neighbors with presents of bass and pickerel and perch from Mink Lake. That was the very neighborly end of the grand winter picnic.

CHAPTER VI.

THE DONATION-PARTY.

One of the first things learned by Susie and Porter Hudson, on their arrival at the farmhouse, had been that the reason why Corry and Pen were not attending school was that the teacher was sick.

"Soon as she's well again," said Pen, "we'll have to go. It's too bad, but she always gets well right away."

Hard as it was, the very next morning after the picnic, word came to the farmhouses all over the valley that school was open.

"Vosh," said his mother, "I can't have ye miss a day, not till you know more'n that there teacher does; and you ort to ketch up with her before the winter's out."

Some little plans of Vosh's, in which his horse and cutter had a part, were upset completely by the teacher's recovery; but the consequences were even more severe at Deacon Farnham's.

90

Corry and Pen were compelled to leave their cousins to take care of themselves every day till after school-hours. It was not so bad for Susie, with her two aunts to care for her. There was the milk-room and the spinning-wheel and the kitchen, and a dozen kinds of knitting to learn, and there were many good books in the house. It looked a little blue to Porter at first, but he faced it manfully. He determined not to spend an hour in the house that he could find a use for out of doors. He went with the deacon to the cattle-yard and the stables, and he learned more about horses and cows and oxen than he had supposed there was to learn.

The sheep, too, were very interesting; especially one old ram that took a dislike to him, and was strongly disposed to drive him out of the sheepfold every time he came in.

Porter discovered, too, that hens, ducks, turkeys, had to live and be cared for in winter as well as in summer; and Susie took a share with him in that part of his work and learning.

All that, and a great deal more, was close around the house; and it was a positive treat to make a trip, after a couple of days, to the forest with his uncle. There was likely to be more snow, the latter said, and he wanted to do all the chopping and hauling he could before the roads should be blocked. Port wondered if it would be possible to burn, before spring,

as much wood as there was already in the woodshed;
but it just suited him to go for more.

The deacon could do the chopping on that and
other days, and Port could be on hand to help him
load the sleigh. The rest of the time, he could be
helping Ponto look for game around among the trees
and bushes.

Between them they bagged some more rabbits,
and once Port actually fired both barrels of his gun
into a covey of partridges.

"Three of 'em?" said his uncle when he brought
them in. "You'll be a sportsman yet, if you keep
on in this way."

That was only three days after the Mink-lake
picnic, and a proud boy was Port when Corry and
Vosh came home. They were not even to have
Saturday to themselves, for there was lost time to
make up over their books.

Aunt Judith said she had never heard of such a
thing when she was young; and Vosh Stebbins went
out to the barn, and sat in his cutter for two hours,
while he worked at his back lessons.

That Sunday they all went to meeting at Benton
Village; and it seemed to Susie Hudson that all she
heard about, except while the minister was preach-
ing, was "the donation." She was not at all sure
but what some of the ladies were thinking of it
during the sermon, from the way they talked about
it afterwards.

"Pen," she said in the sleigh on their way home, "tell me just what it is. I've heard about a donation often enough, but I never saw one."

"Why, don't you know?" exclaimed Pen in great surprise. "Why, a donation — it's a donation : that's all. It's a kind of a picnic at the minister's house. Everybody comes, and they all bring something. Only aunt Judith says some of 'em eat more'n they bring."

"Shall we all go?"

"Of course we will. You'll see. It's the nicest kind of a time."

Susie learned a great deal more during the next two days. Mrs. Farnham and aunt Judith seemed to be cooking for that "donation" as if there were likely to be a famine there, especially in the matter of mince-pies.

"Elder Evans is a real good man," remarked aunt Judith, "but he ain't any kind of a pervider. No, nor his wife ain't either. It won't do to let things go, and have 'em eaten out of house and home."

They were not likely to be, if the rest of the good people in Benton Valley sent over such stores of "goodies" as went to the minister's house, before the day appointed, from Deacon Farnham's.

"I've done my best," said Mrs. Stebbins to Vosh while she was putting her contribution into his cutter for transportation, "but Sarah Farnham and Judith

can beat me. Their oven'll hold three times what
mine will."

She went over early in the afternoon, to help Mrs.
Evans; and she said to Vosh, "You needn't mind
about my gittin' home. I'll come with Judith Farnham."

Perhaps that was why Vosh felt free to say to
Susie Hudson, as she stood at the gate, telling him
how nice his horse and cutter looked, —

"You'll have to go in the deacon's big sleigh with
the rest, but you and I'll have this all to ourselves
coming home."

That was kind of Vosh; and, if there was any
thing Susie was fast learning to like, it was sleighing.

An old-fashioned, up-country donation-party cannot be altogether an evening affair. Some of the
good people have far to come and go, and some of
them have heavy loads to bring: so they generally
begin to assemble before the middle of the afternoon.

Susie had seen the minister's house several times.
It stood in the edge of the village, with an immense
barn behind it; and it looked, for all the world, like
another large barn, painted very white, with ever so
many windows.

"Room," she thought, "for all the company that
will come." And it was a good thing for them
that she was so nearly right. That crowd would
have been very uncomfortable in a small house.

When the sleigh-load from Deacon Farnham's got there, there was already a long line of teams hitched at the roadside in front of the house, beside all that had found shed and stable accommodations here and there.

As for Elder Evans's own barn, hay, straw, and all that sort of thing, formed a regular part of his annual donation. Load after load had come in and been stowed away, after a fashion that spoke well for either the elder's popularity or the goodness of the hay-crop.

There was no intention of letting the good man freeze to death, either, in a country where wood was to be had almost for the chopping. His wood-pile was a sight to see, a good hour before supper, and everybody knew there was more to come.

Corry explained it all to Porter.

"Yes, but he can't eat hay and wood. You say he doesn't get much money."

That was a little after they entered the house, and while Mrs. Farnham and Susie were talking with the elder's kind-faced little wife.

"Eat!" said Corry. "You come right out here with me."

The sitting-room, back of the parlor, was a large one; but it was nearly half full of tables of all sorts and sizes, and these were covered with a feast of such liberal abundance that Porter gave it up at once.

"Even this crowd can't finish all that in one evening, Corry. Will Elder Evans's folks live on what's left, for the rest of the year?"

"Come right along. Vosh is out here. He's one of the receiving committee."

"What's that?"

Corry led his cousin into the kitchen, and a funny-looking place it was. Something like a dozen busy ladies were trying to get at the cook-stove all at the same time; and half as many more were helping Vosh Stebbins "keep track of things," as they were handed in at the side-door, and stowed around in all directions.

"That makes four bushels of onions," Port heard him say, as he and Corry entered the room. "They're a healthy feed — but then!"

"One barrel of flour!" said a tall woman standing near him; "but then, there's ten bushels of wheat."

"Three bags of meal, and twenty sacks of corn; fifteen bushels of turnips, twenty of potatoes; one dressed pig; a side of beef; two dozen chickens."

"Sam Jones has just driven in with another load of wood."

"And Mr. Beans, the miller at Cobbleville, has sent more buckwheat flour'n they can use if they settle down to livin' on flapjacks."

"Five muskrat-skins."

"Two kags of butter."

"Hold on," said Vosh, "till I get down the groceries. Jemimy! What'll he do with so many tallow-dips? and there's more dried apples and doughnuts."

It was indeed a remarkable collection, and Porter began to understand how a "way up country" minister gets his supplies.

"Port," said Corry a little while after that, "let's go for our supper. We want to be ready for the fun."

"What'll that be?"

"Oh, you'll see."

Susie had been making a dreadful mistake at that very moment; for she had asked old Mrs. Jordan, the minister's mother-in-law, if they ever had any dancing at donation-parties. She told Port afterwards that the old lady looked pretty nearly scared to death, and that all she said was, —

"Dancing, child! Sakes alive!"

The house was swarming with young people as well as old, and it was of no manner of use for the leader of the Benton church choir to try and get them all to singing. A hymn or two went off well enough, and then they all listened pretty attentively while a quartet sang some glees. By that time, however, Vosh Stebbins had returned from the kitchen with his list all made up, and ready for the minister; and he said something to another young man, older than himself, but no taller, about "those charades." The music went to the wall, or somewhere else, in about a minute and a half.

Susie Hudson had never heard of one-half the games that followed after the charades. Some of these had been pretty good; but they were hardly noisy enough for the country boys and girls, and in due time were set aside like the music. There were forfeits of several kinds, anagrams, "kiss in the ring," and, after several other things had been proposed and tried, the parlor was given up to a royal game of blind-man's-buff.

It was grand fun for the young people; but, while it went on, there seemed to be every bit as hungry a crowd as ever around the tables in the sitting-room. As fast as any one came out, somebody else went in.

"Deacon Farnham," said Vosh in an undertone, "I've seen that oldest Bean girl eat three suppers already."

" It's a good thing there's plenty."

"Biggest kind of a donation. Sile Hathaway's just got here with two whole deer. Killed 'em on the mountains yesterday."

The deacon brightened up a little as he responded, "Deer, eh? Well, the elder won't starve, anyway."

Susie enjoyed herself exceedingly, but Pen told her, —

"It's real good of you to laugh right out the way you do. They ain't half so much afraid of you now as they were when you got here."

"Afraid of me, Pen?"

"Why, yes : you're a city girl. They ain't a bit afraid of me."

Vosh overheard that, and he added with a broad grin, —

"Fact, Susie. Half these fellows'd rather face a wildcat, any day, than a girl like you, right from the city."

Susie blushed and laughed, but it was a sort of explanation to her of some things she had noticed during the evening.

"Port," said Corry, "let's go out and take a look at Sile Hathaway's deer. One's a buck, and one's a doe, and they're prime."

"Is he a hunter?"

"Guess he is. He'd rather hunt than earn a living, any day. But he's about the best rifle-shot there is anywhere around here."

Port felt that such a man had a great claim to public respect, but he walked on without a word more until they were outside of the kitchen-door.

There on the snow lay the fat doe and the antlered buck, and it made Porter Hudson's very fingers tingle to look on them.

"Where'd you get 'em, Sile?" asked Corry.

"Not more'n a mile up this way from Mink Lake; jest whar the split comes in from towards the old loggin'-camp."

"How'd you get 'em to the village?"

"Well, of course I had my pony along. Allers do. Made a pole-drag right thar. I had two more deer to fetch in, and they wasn't more'n jest a good load for a drag."

He was a long, lanky, grizzled sort of man, with keen gray eyes, and a stoop in his shoulders.

"What's a pole-drag?" asked Port.

"Why," replied Corry, "all he does is to cut down two saplings, and make a kind of sled of 'em. It won't last long, but it'll do to haul deer home. I'll show you one to-morrow."

Port would have stood and looked at the deer longer if the weather out there had been warmer, but he half made up his mind to be a hunter while he was feeling of that buck's antlers. There was something magnetic about them that sent a hunting-fever all over him.

At last the pleasant gathering at the minister's house began to break up. Some sleigh-loads of those who had far to go had already set out for their homes, and it was well understood that not even the village people and near neighbors would stay later than ten o'clock. Very likely Elder Evans and his family would be tired enough to be pleased at once more having their home to themselves.

There came at the end a trifle of a surprise to Susie Hudson. The country-boys grew bolder as breaking-up time drew near; and she was compelled to inform no less than three of them in succession, when they offered her a ride home in their own cutters, that she was already supplied with company.

She did not happen to see Vosh Stebbins's triumphant grin at one of these young men when he was turning away to hunt for another girl, but she better understood why her thoughtful young neighbor had spoken to her beforehand.

She learned yet one thing more before she arrived at her uncle's house. That was, that there were two roads to it, and the one selected by Vosh for the return drive was several times longer than that by which Deacon Farnham had driven his big sleigh. The snowy track was everywhere in fine condition; the sorrel colt was in the best of spirits; the bells rang out clearly in a ceaseless jingle as the gay little turnout dashed along: it was altogether a capital winding-up for an evening of genuine "winter fun" in the country.

There was a great deal of merry talk in the larger sleigh all the way home. The older people, Mrs. Stebbins included, were in a good state of mind over the success of the party, and Pen had something to say about everybody she had seen.

"Corry," said Port as he nestled down among the buffalo-robes, "is there any thing up this way that pays better than a donation?"

"I don't know. Tell you what, though: they say we're to have a big spelling-match in about two weeks."

"What's that?"

"Why, it's this way: the Benton school-district takes in all the young folks around here. The Cobbleville school-district joins ours, only it's bigger, and there's more of 'em. We're to spell against 'em. It's tip-top fun; but I'm awfully afraid they'll spell us down. They did last year, and the year before."

"Can Susie and I go?"

"Of course you can. We've a right to count in anybody that's living in our district."

"I'm in, then. I live here."

"Will Susie come? She ought to be a good speller. The day isn't set yet. They were talking it over to-night. We'll have to go to Cobbleville: they've got the biggest meeting-house."

"Meeting-house? What for?"

"Why, to hold the match in. It'll be jam full, too, galleries and all. Everybody comes out to a spelling-match. You'll see."

Port had no end of questions to ask; but he felt

that he was becoming a country-boy very fast, and that he already had a strong interest in upholding the honor of the Benton school-district.

"Susie?" he said. "Why, of course she'll go. She can spell any thing."

CHAPTER VII.

THE WORD-BATTLE AT COBBLEVILLE.

PENELOPE was in bed and asleep when Susie returned from the donation. So long a road home as Vosh Stebbins had selected, had required time to travel over it; and Mrs. Farnham had vetoed Pen's proposal to sit up. When they all reached the breakfast-table in the morning, there was a great deal to talk about, but it was not long before the spelling-match came up.

"Oh, yes! Susie," said Pen, "I was going to tell you all about it. You know how to spell."

"They say we can be counted in among the Benton spellers," began Port; but there was a very serious look on Susie's face as she said to him, —

"I promised to go; but then, to think of being spelled down!"

"Why, Susie!" exclaimed Pen, "where did you hear of it?"

"Wasn't she at the donation?" asked Corry.

104

"Didn't she ride home with Vosh Stebbins? Guess she's heard as much as anybody."

That was not a bad guess; but it soon appeared that Susie was as much in earnest over the results of the match as if she were a regular Benton-valley settler, instead of a mere visitor.

There was plenty of enthusiasm warming up, but Deacon Farnham seemed inclined to throw cold water on their hope of victory. He reminded them of the disastrous manner in which their district champions had already been defeated twice in succession.

"They've had a pretty good teacher, too, all winter," he said.

"So've we," said Corry; "and some of us have been putting in on our spelling more'n any thing else."

"That's good. Maybe they have too. I shouldn't wonder if Vosh was the best man you've got."

"Perhaps he is, and perhaps he isn't. Anyhow, we're going to have fair play this time. Their teacher isn't going to put out the words. There'll be a committee."

"That's better; but I'm afraid there won't be any prize brought back to this valley."

"It's a splendid prize!" exclaimed Pen, — "a great big dixinary."

"A dictionary, eh?"

"Yes," said Port; "and all the words spelled are to be given out from it."

"Any kind of words?"

"Not exactly. They must be just such words as people use, but they can be as long as they can find in the book."

"That won't hurt one side more'n it will the other," said Mrs. Farnham.

"Besides," said Pen, "more of us had to sit down on short words than long ones last year."

"Sit down?" asked Port.

"When they missed. You'll see when you get there," replied Corry. "It's awful to sit down on a mistake, with a whole meeting-house full of people looking at you and laughing."

"I should say it was."

There were four pairs of eyes in that one house, right away after breakfast, busy over the long rows of words in some spelling-books, and wondering if there were any there they had forgotten.

"I knew 'em all once," said Pen; "but they always look different when you're told 'em from the pulpit."

Over at the Stebbins homestead it was very much the same.

"Vosh," said his mother, "you was a dreadful long time at the barn."

"Well, mother, I staid till I'd spelled over every thing I could see. There's a good many names to

things around a stable, and I spelled every one
of 'em."

"Did you git 'em right, Vosh?"

"Guess I did."

"Would it do ye any good to have some other kind
of spellin'-book, so you'd know more words?"

"That isn't the trouble, mother. It kind o' seems
to me I know so many now, I can't remember half
of 'em."

"Don't you git spelled down, now, Vosh. You
won't, will ye, not with Susie Hudson and her
brother a-lookin' on?"

Vosh's face put on a pretty sober expression as
he muttered, —

"Guess I wouldn't like that."

The quiet winter days went by rapidly, and nothing came in them to interrupt in any way the
steadily growing excitement over the great spelling-
match.

All the arrangements for it were discussed over
and over, until at last there was nothing more to be
settled, and the set day came.

"Corry," said Port, when the sleigh drove to the
door after supper, and they were hurrying on their
overcoats, "seems to me I couldn't spell the shortest
word I ever heard."

"If you get scared, you'll miss, sure's you live.
Now, Port, we've just got to beat 'em."

Vosh and his cutter came up at that moment, and Mrs. Stebbins stepped out with the remark, —

"Deacon, you must make room for me. I'll swop with Susie. I want a talk with Judith and Sarah."

"Come, Susie," said Vosh. "I've been teaching my colt to spell."

There was no spare room in the big sleigh, for the farmhouse was left in charge of Ponto and the hired man.

Mrs. Farnham and aunt Judith would not for any thing have missed hearing for themselves how Penelope and Coriolanus, and Susie and Porter, managed their long words at Cobbleville.

The red cutter was jingling away down the road before the black span was in motion, but somehow the two sets of passengers reached Cobbleville at about the same time. Eight miles of excellent sleighing does not last long before fast horses, and there was to be no such thing as being late.

"This is Cobbleville, Susie."

"It's not so much bigger than Benton. I don't believe we shall be beaten."

Something like that same suggestion cheered up Porter Hudson a little, as the deacon drove into the village; but the faces of Pen and Corry were very serious. There was a great trial before them, and they knew it, — a very great trial; for the tall-steepled, white-painted meeting-house in the middle of the village-green was hardly large enough to hold the crowd which was now pouring into it. The people had come from miles and miles all over the country; and those of the Cobbleville district were not only the more numerous, but seemed to be in a sort of exultation over a victory they were sure to win.

Deacon Farnham and his party managed to secure seats, and then they could look around them. Up on the platform, behind the pulpit-desk, were several very dignified gentlemen; and it did the Benton people good to see Elder Evans among them.

"He's come to see fair play," whispered Corry. "He won't let 'em put out any words they ought not to. Our chance is good."

That was encouraging; and at that very moment Elder Evans arose, and came forward to say to his own parishioners, —

"Some of our friends of the Cobbleville district have visitors among their young people, and the committee have consented to their taking part in the exercises."

"That fixes you and Susie all right," said Corry. "They can't object to you now."

Of course not; and the other final arrangements were speedily completed.

It was simple enough, or would have been if there had not been so many boys and girls who had not learned to stand still. The pews and the galleries, all but a few of the very forward pews, were given up to the general public.

The young folk from the Benton district were made to stand in the right-hand aisle, in a line that reached from the platform to the door. The other aisle belonged to Cobbleville, and its line of spellers came near being a double one.

"Two to our one, Port," said Corry; "but they'll thin out fast enough after we begin to spell."

There was no such thing as selecting places at first. The spelling began at the head of each line, alternating from one to the other. If the speller missed, he or she sat down wherever a seat could be found; but, as fast as words were spelled rightly, their happy victors were entitled to march to the heads of their lines, and so these were kept continually in motion. It was a proud thing to walk up the whole length of that meeting-house again and again, but it was not so proud to walk down the aisle hunting for a seat.

"I see how it is," said Port.

"Yes, it's great fun; and the last one up gets the dictionary."

It had been agreed that neither of the school-teachers should give out the words, and Elder Evans had modestly insisted that the pastor of the Cobbleville church should perform that duty.

"Won't he kill 'em off, though!" exclaimed Corry dolefully.

"Won't he play fair?"

"Why, yes, he'll be honest enough, I s'pose. But then he pronounces so! Wait till you hear him."

It was about time to begin, and the two boys and Pen found themselves quite a little distance down the line below Vosh and Susie.

"That's Elder Keyser. Oh, but isn't that a big dictionary! Hush! he's giving out a word."

Nobody needed to be told that, for it was given in a deep, very heavy voice, that was heard all over the house; but Port at once understood all about Elder Keyser's pronunciation.

The poor word was in a manner tumbled neck and heels out of the good man's mouth, with a sort of vocal kick to hurry it; and there were chances of serious injury to any syllable that should happen to stumble.

"Hypocrite!" shouted the elder to the curly-headed youngster at the head of the Cobbleville line.

"H-i-p" —

"That'll do. Give an example, and take your seat."

"Example," piped the boy, "puttin' a bad cent in the contribution-box."

"Next. Hypocrite."

The bright little girl at the head of the Benton

aisle spelled it correctly, and Elder Evans raised his
head high to smile on her.

The words were now given out with something
like rapidity; and there was a constant stream of
boys and girls walking up the aisles, and of others
coming in the opposite directions. Every one of the
latter seemed to be muttering, —

"I knew that word just as well!"

It was well that the front pews had been kept for
unlucky spellers; but a seat in one of them was
hardly looked upon as a prize.

"Port," said Corry gleefully, "they're thinning out
fast. Think of a girl and two boys going down on
such a word as 'rotation'!"

"Was that it? I thought he said 'rundition;'
and I'd never seen it anywhere. He'll stumble me,
sure's you live."

It was nearly their turn; and they one after the
other felt a ton or so lighter when they were able
to march to the front, instead of going to find seats.

Before that, however, Elder Keyser had thrown as
hard a word as he could find at the head of Vosh
Stebbins.

"Glad he had to say it slow," thought Vosh.
"Guess he never tried it before. I can do it."

He was safe for the time, and the next Cobbleville
boy went down on an easy word that then came
across to Susie. She was conscious of a great deal

of red in her face; but she spelled it clearly and correctly, and that sent her to the head, and next to Vosh again.

Twice more around, and the lines of young people in the aisles were not nearly so long as at first.

There had been, moreover, an almost continual roar of laughter over the examples of use given by the unfortunates.

Hardly were Port and Corry safe on the second round, before Elder Keyser blurted out to the next boy a word that sounded like —

"Ber'l."

"Bar'l, b-a-r-r" —

"That'll do. Example?"

"A bar'l of flour."

"Next. Ber'l."

"Ber'l, b-e-r-y-l."

"Down. Wrong. Example?"

"Beryl, a precious stone;" and the blushing damsel sorrowfully slipped aside into one of the front pews.

"Next. Ber'l."

"Berril, b-u-r-r-i-a-l."

"Wrong. Down. Example?"

"Berril, the berril of Surgeon Moore. I've heerd 'em sing it."

That boy sat down; but the young lady opposite spelled "burial" correctly, even if she pronounced it "burriel."

Once more round ; and now Cobbleville could show barely twenty, and the Benton district hardly a baker's dozen.

"We're getting 'em," chuckled Corry. "They've lost some of their best spellers on old Keyser's pronunciation."

Alas for Corry! His turn came to him next upon a word the sound of which he was sure he caught.

"Stood, s-t-oo-d."

"Wrong. Down. Example?"

"Stewed, then!" roared Corry in undisguised vexation. "Example: 'The boy stewed on the burning deck.'"

"Next." The word sounded a little shorter this time ; and the Cobbleville champion, whose turn it was, began, —

"Stud, s-t-u-d."

"Wrong. Down. Example?"

"One of my shirt-studs;" and down he went in a great roar of laughter, while Porter Hudson took the hint Corry's "example" had given him, and went to the head again on "stewed."

The rounds went by rapidly now ; and each one sent down somebody in disgrace, while the excitement of the audience was visibly increasing.

"Susie," whispered Vosh, "we've got as many left standing as they have. Keyser's killing 'em off fast, though."

"That's what I'm afraid of."

"Don't spell a word till you know what it is, even if you have to ask him."

"I'd never dare do that."

"I would, then."

She was just above him, and in another moment her trial came. Vosh saw the puzzled, troubled expression on her face, and he came to the rescue.

"Elder Keyser," he sang out, "was that word 'mystery,' or 'mastery,' or 'monastery,' or was it 'mercy'? There's a difference in the spelling of 'em."

"Silence!"

"Silence, s-i-l-e-n-c-e," gravely spelled Susie, while the whole meeting-house rang with the applause that greeted her.

"Next. Spell 'misery,'" sharply exclaimed Elder Keyser; and a very pretty young lady of Cobbleville was so far disconcerted by the suddenness of it, that she actually began, —

"Misery, m-i-z" —

"Wrong. Down. Example?"

"Misery — ah! nothing to eat."

Susie was safe for that round; and in the next Elder Keyser was almost spitefully slow and correct in uttering the word he gave her.

During all that time, the older people from the farmhouse had been watching the course of events with no small degree of exultation over the success of their young representatives.

Corry had joined them, and about his first remark was, —

"Oh, but won't old Keyser be a popular man in Cobbleville after to-night! He'd better go in for a donation. Half the boys in the village'd like to snowball him on his way home."

The game grew closer. Barely six on a side, when Corry exclaimed, —

"That cross-eyed girl's down! She was the best speller they had last year. Too bad, too. She spelled 'bunch,' when what old Keyser said was 'bench.' It's a good deal too much to have to guess at what's in his mouth, and then spell it."

"Dear, dear!" exclaimed aunt Judith a moment later. "Here comes Pen."

"Such luck she's had!" said Corry. "Nothing harder than 'melon' since she began. Now it's Port's turn. Here he comes."

"Port," said Mrs. Farnham, "what was that word?"

"'Baratry,' and I thought he said 'battery;' and that long-necked Cobbleville boy said 'bartery,' and gave 'swopping jackknives' for an example."

It could not last much longer now.

"There!" exclaimed Mrs. Stebbins, "if my Vosh ain't all alone on our side! O Lavawjer!"

"O Susie!" groaned Port, "to think of her spelling 'elopement' without any middle 'e'!"

She had done it by a slip of the tongue, and, when asked for an example, stammered out, —

"Elopement, a runaway," and left Vosh to fight what there was left of Cobbleville. There would have been three against him, if a bright boy had not forgotten how many "l's" there should be in "traveller," and then given himself for an example as he shot away down the aisle.

Vosh knew how to spell "traveller;" and the next word went across the house to be spelled as "porringer," when all the elder wanted was "porridge."

"Two left," said Mrs. Stebbins, — "that there dumpy gal and my Vosh."

"She's one of the smartest girls in all Cobbleville," said Corry.

"She ain't as smart as my Vosh."

Opinions might vary on a point like that; and every time the healthy-looking young lady whom Mrs. Stebbins so unkindly described as "dumpy" spelled a word correctly, her conduct was approved by Cobbleville in a rousing round of applause. All that Vosh's friends could do for him was as nothing to it, but he had his revenge. On the fourth word, after they were left alone, the applause began too soon.

The healthy young lady remembered too well the

nature of Susie Hudson's blunder, and she rashly inserted an unnecessary " e " in "fusibility."

"Wrong. Down. Example?"

" Fusibility — example ! " — a long, confused hesitation — "butter, sir."

And the hasty multitude of Cobbleville had been loudly cheering the unlucky " e " which the triumphant Vosh the next moment very carefully omitted.

Didn't Benton cheer then !

"Vosh has got the dictionary!" all but shouted his happy mother. "I declare, I'll read it through."

"If she does," whispered Corry to Port, " she'll never stop talking again as long as she lives."

" She'd have all the words she'd need to keep her a-going."

The ceremony of presenting the prize was gracefully turned over to Elder Evans by his reverend friend and the committee. The good man seemed to take a special pleasure in delivering so very large a book to "a young member of his own flock," as he expressed it. It must be confessed that Vosh looked more than a little "sheepish" when he walked forward, and held out his hands for the prize.

The great spelling-match was over, and the crowd of old and young spectators began to disperse.

Before the Cobbleville boys could make up their minds clearly whether it was their duty to snowball Elder Keyser or the Benton-district folk, the latter were mostly on their way home.

"Susie," said Vosh, as he stowed the dictionary carefully away in the red cutter, "I wish you'd won it."

"I'm real glad I didn't, then. Our side beat, and that's quite enough for me."

CHAPTER VIII.

AN OLD-FASHIONED SNOW.

THERE had been several light and fleecy falls of snow since the arrival of the "city cousins" at the farmhouse, but they had been only about enough to keep the sleighing in good order. The weather was bracingly cold; but, for all that, aunt Judith more than once felt called upon to remark, —

"The winters nowadays ain't nothin' at all to what they used to be."

"We'll have more snow yet," said the deacon. "Don't you be afraid."

"Snow, Joshaway! Well, if you've forgotten, I haven't. I've seen this place of ourn jest snowed in for days and days, so't you couldn't git to the village at all till the roads was broke."

Mrs. Stebbins had had a great deal more to say about it, all in the same strain; and the only consolation seemed to be, in the language of Deacon Farnham, —

"It's the best kind of a winter for the lumbermen. The choppers haven't had to lose a day of time, and the haulin's the best you ever heard tell of."

Just snow enough, and no more. That sort of thing was not to be securely counted on, however, as they were all about to learn. The very Saturday after the spelling-match, the morning opened with a sort of haze creeping over the north-eastern sky.

It seemed to drift down from somewhere among the mountains, and by noon the snow began to fall.

"Boys," said the deacon, "it's going to be a big one this time, real old-fashioned sort. We must get out the shovels, and keep the paths open."

It hardly seemed necessary to do any shovelling yet; but the white flakes fell faster and faster, hour after hour, and night came on earlier than usual.

"Now, Port," said Corry, "if you and I know what's good for ourselves, we'll lay in all the wood we'll need for to-morrow and next day. Every thing'll be snowed clean under."

"That's so, but I wouldn't ha' missed seeing it come."

Neither would Susie; and she and Pen watched it from the sitting-room windows, while even aunt Judith came and stood beside them, and declared, —

"There, now, that's something like;" and Mrs. Farnham remarked in a tone of exultation, —

"You never saw any thing like that in the city, Susie."

"Never, aunt Sarah. It's splendid. It's the grandest snow-storm I ever heard of."

There was very little wind as yet, and the fluttering flakes lay still where they fell.

"All the snow that couldn't get down before is coming now," said Pen. "There's ever so much of it. I like snow."

More and more of it; and the men and boys came in from the barns after supper as white as so many polar bears, to stamp and laugh and be brushed till the color of their clothes could be seen.

Then the wind began to rise, and the whole family felt like gathering closely around the fireplace; and the flames poured up the wide chimney as if they were ready to fight that storm.

The boys cracked nuts, and popped corn, and played checkers. The deacon read his newspaper. Mrs. Farnham and aunt Judith plied their knitting. Susie showed Pen how to crochet a tidy. It was very cosey and comfortable; but all the while they could hear blast after blast, as they came howling around the house, and hurled the snow fiercely against the windows.

"Isn't it grand?" said Port at last. "But we'll have some shovelling to do in the morning."

"Guess we will!"

"And you'll have a good time getting to school."

"School! If this keeps on all night, there won't be any going to meeting to-morrow, let alone school on Monday."

It did keep on all night; and the blinding drifts were whirling before the wind with a gustier sweep than ever, when the farmhouse people peered out at them next morning.

Every shovel they could furnish a pair of hands for had to be at work good and early, and the task before them had a kind of impossible look about it.

The cattle and sheep and horses had all been carefully sheltered. Even the poultry had received special attention from their human protectors. They were all sure to be found safe and warm, but the difficulty now was in finding them at all.

There was a drift nearly ten feet high between the house and the pigpen, and a worse one was piled up over the gate leading into the barnyard.

How those pigs did squeal, while they impatiently waited for the breakfast which was so very long in coming!

"They're nearest, father," said Corry. "Hadn't we better stop that noise, first thing we do?"

"You and Port go for them."

They dug away manfully at that drift, or, rather, at the hole they meant to make through it, while the grown-up shovellers toiled in the direction of the barnyard-gate.

"Corry," said Port, "don't you think this is pretty hard work for Sunday morning?"

"Those pigs don't know any thing about Sunday. The cows don't either. They get hungry, just the same."

"I s'pose it's all right."

"Right! You trust father for that. He says the Lord made Sunday, and the Lord sent the snow, and we needn't worry about it. The Lord wants all his cattle fed regularly."

"Did your father say that?"

"Yes, I heard him saying it to aunt Judith."

"It's all right, then. But don't you think it's pretty hard work for any kind of day?"

"Yes, but it's fun. Hear those pigs! They know we're coming."

It sounded a great deal as if the hungry quadrupeds in the pen were explaining their condition to all the outside world, or trying to, and cared very little how much work it might cost to bring them their breakfast.

Their neighbors in the stables and barn made less fuss about the matter, but they had even longer to wait. Before the great drift at the gate could be conquered, it was breakfast-time for human beings, and there was never a morning when coffee and hot cakes seemed more perfectly appropriate.

While the human workers were busy at the break-

fast-table, the snow and wind did not take any resting spell, but kept right on, doing their best to
restore the damaged drifts.

"Susie," said Port, "doesn't this make you think
of Lapland?"

"Or Greenland, or Siberia?"

"Tell you what," said Corry, "I don't believe the
Russians get any thing much better than this."

"If they do," said aunt Judith, "I don't want to
live there. There won't be any going to meeting
to-day."

"Meeting!" exclaimed the deacon. "There'll be
a dozen big drifts between this and the village. All
hands'll have to turn out to breaking roads, soon as
the storm lets up."

No end of it was reached that day; but the barn
was reached, and all the quadrupeds and bipeds
were found, safe and hungry, and were carefully attended to.

"We sha'n't get into the woods again right away,"
said Corry; and he was right about that, but there
was a thoughtful look on Susie's face as she remarked, —

"I wonder how Mrs. Stebbins is getting along.
There's nobody there but Vosh."

"He's a worker," said the deacon. "He's very
strong for his age, — likeliest youngster in the whole
valley. We can't get over there to-day, but we will
to-morrow."

That had indeed been a busy time for Vosh, hard and late as he had worked the night before; and his mother came out to help him.

"It ain't no time to talk, Lavawjer," she said to him; "but I do wish I knowed how the deacon's folks was a-gettin' on. They must be pretty nigh snowed under."

"Guess they're all right, but it'll give Susie and Port some notion of what snow can do in the country."

Away on into the night the great northern gusts worked steadily; but towards morning it seemed as if the storm decided that it had done enough, and it began to subside. Now and then it again took hold as if it had still a drift or so to finish; but by sunrise every thing was still and calm and wonderfully white.

"This'll be a working-day, I guess," said the deacon; "but all the paths we make'll stay made."

There was some comfort in that; for all they had made on Sunday had to be shovelled out again, and the pigs were as noisy as ever.

The deacon insisted on digging out every gate so it would swing wide open; and all the paths were made wide and clear, walled high on either side with tremendous banks of snow. It was after dinner, and the workers were getting a little weary of it, before they could open the front-gate.

Susie was watching them from the windows, and

Pen was in the front-yard, vigorously punching a snow-bank with a small shovel, when aunt Judith suddenly exclaimed right over Susie's shoulder, —

"Sakes alive! There's somethin' a-stirrin' in the road. What can it be? — Sarah, call to Joshaway! There's a human critter out there in the snow."

Susie almost held her breath, for there was surely a commotion in the great drift a few rods beyond the gate. The boys saw it too, and they and the deacon and the hired man began to shout, as if shouting would help a fellow in a deep snow.

"Father," said Corry, "shall we go and see who it is?"

"Not as long as he can thrash around like that. He'll get through."

"He's gone away under," said Port. "There he comes — no, he's under again. It's awful deep."

"He'll be smothered."

Susie was watching that commotion in the snow as she had never watched any thing before, and just then a fleecy head came out on this side of the high drift.

"Aunt Judith! — Aunt Sarah! — It's Vosh Stebbins!"

"They're all snowed under, and he's come through to tell us. Oh, dear!"

"Hurrah, boys!"

There was nothing at all doleful in the ringing

shout Vosh sent towards the house the moment he got the snow out of his mouth.

"Have you got any snow at your house? There's more'n we want up our way. Let ye have loads of it, and not charge a cent."

"Come on, Vosh," said the deacon. "How'd you find the roads?"

"Sleighin' enough to last all summer, if you don't waste it. More like swimming than walking."

"I'd say it was. Come on in and warm yourself."

Both the boys were brushing the snow from him as soon as he got to the gate, and all the women-folk were out on the stoop to welcome him. Aunt Judith talked as fast as his own mother could have done, and insisted on his sitting down before the fireplace while she brought him a cup of coffee, and a glass of currant-wine, and a piece of pie, and then she said she would make him some pepper-tea.

"Now, Miss Farnham," said Vosh, "I ain't hurt a bit."

"And your mother?"

"Never was better; but she was worried about you folks, and I said I'd come over and see. — Susie, did you know it'd been snowing a little out of doors?"

"How did you ever get through?"

"I just burrowed most of the way, like a wood-chuck."

"You can't go back by the same hole," chuckled Corry.

"I could if it was there. Guess I won't stay long, though : mother'll be afraid I'm lost in the drift."

He was right about that ; and, after a few minutes of merry talk, they all gathered at the front-gate to see him plunge in again.

"He'll get through," said the deacon. "There's the makin' of a man in Vosh. He goes right straight ahead into any thing."

The last thing he had said before starting was, —

"'All Benton Valley'll be out a-breakin' roads to-morrow."

"That's so," said the deacon ; but, after Vosh had gone, he added, "and snow-ploughs won't be of any kind of use."

"How'll we work it ?" said Corry.

"Teams and sleds. It'll be a tough job, and the roads'll be pretty rough for a while."

"Corry," said Port, "how'll they do it, — cart the snow away ?"

"Where'd they cart it to? You just wait and see."

They were all tired enough to go to bed early, but the first rays of daylight next morning saw them all rushing out again. Port felt a little stiff and sore, but he determined to do his part at road-breaking.

The snow lay pretty level in the roads, for the

greater part ; and you could see the top rails of the fences here and there, enough to go by.

A little after breakfast the wide gate was swung open, and then the deacon's hired man came down the lane, driving the black team at a sharp trot, with the wood-sleigh behind them.

Faster, faster, through the gate, and out into the snow, with a chorus of shouts to urge them on.

The spirited, powerful fellows reared and plunged and snorted ; but before long they seemed almost disposed to call it fun, and enjoy it.

"Up the road first !" shouted the deacon. "We'll break that way till we get beyond Stebbins's."

There was work for men and boys, as well as horses ; and the snow-shovels were plied rapidly behind the plunging team. Porter Hudson quickly understood that a great deal of road could be opened in such a way as that, if all the farmers turned out to do it. They were likely to ; for none of them could afford to be blocked in, and public opinion would have gone pretty sharply against any man who dodged his share of such important work as that.

It was hardest on the horses, willingly as they went at it ; and at the end of an hour or so the deacon brought out his second team, a pair of strong brown plough-horses. When they were tired, out came the best yoke of oxen ; and it was fun enough to see the great, clumsy creatures, all but buried in a deep drift, slowly but strongly shouldering their way forward, and every now and then trying to turn around and get out of the scrape.

"A skittish yoke wouldn't do," said Corry. "They wouldn't move any way but backwards."

Long before that, the road had been opened "beyond Stebbins's," and Vosh had joined them with his snow-shovel. His paths were all in a condition that spoke well for his industry, and the deacon told him so. Mrs. Stebbins was at the gate, and she remarked, —

"Tell ye what, deacon, if you think my Vosh can't do any thing but spell for dixinaries, you're mistaken. He's a worker, he is."

"That's so."

But there was no need of his saying much more, for there in the road behind him were Mrs. Farnham and aunt Judith, and Susie and Pen ; and you could have heard every voice among them, till the front-door shut behind the last one.

That was Pen, and her last word had been a shout to Vosh in the road : —

"We've got more snow in our front-yard than you have, anyhow."

They were now pushing their work towards the village, and could already catch glimpses of other "gangs," as Vosh called them, here and there down the road. In some places, where the snow was not so deep, they made "turnouts" wide enough for loaded sleighs to pass each other.

"If we didn't," said Vosh, "one team'd have to lie down and let the other drive over it."

He could not tell Port that he had ever seen that done, but he added, "I've had to burrow through a drift, team and all, when there wasn't any turnout made."

That was very much like what they had been doing all day, and they kept it up through all the next; but, when Tuesday night came, it was pretty clear that "the roads were open." A sleigh came up from Benton with a man in it who had business with the deacon, and who had some remarkable yarns to tell about the depth of the drifts on the other side of the valley.

"Deacon Paulding's house was just drifted clean under, barns and all. He had to make a kind of a tunnel to his stable, before he could fodder his critters."

"You don't say!" exclaimed aunt Judith. "Snowed under! I've known that to happen any number of times when I was a girl. Good big houses too; not little hencoops of things, like that there house of old Deacon Paulding's. He's a small specimen too. He'd need a tunnel to git through most any thin'. I must say, though, this 'ere's a right good old-fashioned snow, to come in these days."

It was new-fashioned enough to Porter and Susie, and the former remarked, —

"Oh, but won't there be some water when all this begins to melt ! "

Others were thinking of that very thing, for the sun had been very bright all day. It was brighter still on the day that followed ; and towards night a dull, leaden fog arose in the west, for the sun to go down in.

"Father," said Mrs. Farnham, "do you think there's more snow coming ? "

"Guess not, Sarah. It looks more like a rain and a thaw."

"There's most always a thaw in February, but it 'pears as if it was a little early in the month."

So it was, and the weather made a sort of failure for once. To be sure, there were several hours next day when the winter seemed to have let go its hold, and while a dull, slow, cold rain came pouring down upon the snow-drifts. They settled under it a little sullenly, and then the wind shifted to the north-east, and it grew cold enough for anybody.

"I've known it to do that very thing when I was a girl," said aunt Judith. "There'll be the awfullest kind of a crust."

"Glad we had all our breaking done before this came," said her brother. "It'd be heavy work to do now."

The hard frost of that night was followed by a crisp and bracing morning, and aunt Judith's prophecy was fulfilled. The crust over the great snow-fall was strong enough to bear the weight of a man almost anywhere.

"Hurrah!" shouted Corry, as he climbed a drift, and walked away towards the open field beyond. "We'll have some fun now."

"What kind of fun?" asked Port.

"What kind? Well, all kinds, — sliding down hill, snow-shoeing in the woods, all sorts of things."

"Hurrah for all that!"

"Boys!" shouted Vosh from the front-gate, "the mill-pond was flooded yesterday, and it's frozen hard now. There's acres and acres of the best skating you ever heard of, glary as a pane of glass."

There was a shout then that brought aunt Judith and Susie to the window, and Porter was saying to himself, —

"Well, I am glad we brought along our skates, after all. There'll be a chance to use 'em."

CHAPTER IX.

GRAND COASTING.

VOSH STEBBINS got home from school very early Friday afternoon, and his chores were attended to in a great hurry.

After that, his mother's mind was stirred to the curiosity point by an unusual amount of hammering out in the barn. He was a good deal of a mechanical genius, or, as she expressed it, "he had a nateral turn for tools;" and he had more than once astonished her by the results of his hammering. When, however, she asked him what he was up to, all she could get from him was, —

"I tell you what, mother, I'm going to show 'em a new wrinkle. Wait till morning. 'Tisn't quite ready yet."

"You'd ort to tell me, Vosh. Mebbe I could give you some idees."

He was very close-mouthed for once, however, and it may be he had some doubts about his own "idees."

135

The Benton boys and girls had not learned to say "coasting:" they all called it "sliding down hill." But the country they lived in had been planned expressly for it. The hills around the valley were steeper in some places than in others, but the roads generally had to wind more or less in climbing them. There was not enough of travelling on any of them to interfere seriously with the free use of sleds, and you could almost always see whether or not the track was clear. Just now, however, the very depth of the snow was in the way, for the heavy sleighs had cut down into it so as to leave great ridges in the middle. That was enough to spoil the running of any thing narrow. The great storm, therefore, would have been a bad thing in that connection, but for the thaw and freeze, and the splendid, thick, icy crust.

Not more than a mile east of Deacon Farnham's, the land sloped down almost gently for more than a mile, to the very edge of the village; and there were roads from that on, to the borders of the little river and the mill-pond. Of course all that slope was not in one field; but all the low and broken fences were now snowed under, and it was easy to take the top rails from the two or three high ones, so as to leave wide gaps. With very little trouble, therefore, the boys prepared for their fun a clear, slippery descent, almost level in some places, that would have been hard to beat anywhere. The hollows were all drifted full, and there was a good road on one side to go up hill by. All that had been duly explained to Susie and Port by Corry, and their great affliction seemed to be that they only had one sled among them.

"It'll hold you and me, Port, if we stick on hard; besides, we can take turns."

"And I'll slide Susie," said Pen.

Susie had very little to say about it during the evening; but the idea grew upon her all the time, and she went out to look at Corry's sled in the morning, after breakfast. Aunt Judith stood in the doorway, and heard her say, —

"Yes, it must be splendid!"

"Why, Susie Hudson! That sort of rompin', tomboy business ain't for grown-up young ladies."

"I'm not grown-up, aunt Judith: I'm only sixteen."

"Goin' on seventeen, and you're from the city too; and that there mite of a sled — well, it's good enough for boys."

Just then Corry sang out, —

"Halloo, Vosh! Going to slide down hill in a cutter?"

There he was at the gate, sorrel colt, red blanket, bells, and all.

"Cutter! No; but you wouldn't have the girls walk up hill after every slide, would you?"

"The girls!" exclaimed aunt Judith. "They ain't a-goin'. I won't hear to any sech thing."

"Now, Miss Farnham, you come out here and look at my sled. They've got one like it over in Cobbleville, only mine's bigger. If you'll come along with us" —

"Me come! Sakes alive! But what have you been a-doin'?"

"Why, Vosh," said Corry, "it's your little old pair of bobs, and you've rigged a box on the hind one. What's that in front?"

"That's my rudder."

"Rudder! You can't steer with it: a rudder ought to be behind."

"Ought it, now? Don't you see? The front bob turns on a pin in the middle, that comes up through the centre plank. I've greased it, so it turns easy. See how I've rigged that yoke to the front bob? See the two arms a-standing up? You pull on one of those arms, and you pull around the head of the bob. That steers 'em. The hind bob follows the front one: can't help it, if it tries."

Aunt Judith walked all around it: she even gave one arm of that yoke a hard push to see if it would really turn the "bob" sled it was geared to.

"Sakes alive! It'll do it!"

Susie had hardly waited to say good-morning to Vosh; and there she was now, with her hood on, exclaiming, —

"Pen, Pen! why don't you go and get your things on? We mustn't keep Vosh waiting."

Pen was off like a flash, and Corry remarked to Vosh, —

"That'll be just great, if it'll work."

"Work! It's sure to work. It's as good as the Cobbleville 'ripper.' That's what they call it. All it wants is somebody strong in the arms to steer."

"I'd never trust myself," said aunt Judith with a deep sigh of anxiety.

"Tell you what, Corry," said Port, "we'll make Vosh haul us up hill. Won't have to walk."

"That's the checker. First time I ever had a horse and a man to help me slide down hill."

They discovered afterwards how important a part of the sport that was; but just then they all had to join in begging permission for Susie and Pen to go. Even Mrs. Farnham had her objections, and the deacon himself was studying the matter; when down the road came Mrs. Stebbins, and the case was won for the young people.

"Judith," she asked, "wasn't you and Sarah ever no younger'n you be now? It does seem to me as if some folks forgot they was ever gals and boys, and slid down hill, and had a good time, and wasn't a mite the worse for it. Vosh, he's been a-hammerin' away at that thing till he jest knows it'll work, and so do I. — Susie, you and Pen git right into the

cutter, and I'll explain how them bobs'll steer. You
see " —

"Get in, Pen," said the deacon. "Get in, Susie.
— Don't you try too heavy a load, Vosh."

"Joshaway, they'll break all their precious necks."

"No, they won't. I'll risk it."

"Judith," went on Mrs. Stebbins, "I'll tell ye all
about it;" and that was what she was yet doing,
after the cutter turned the corner of the road below
the house, with the ripper behind it, and Port and
Corry on their sled, dragging joyously astern of the
new invention.

The whole country was icy, and glittered beauti-
fully white, in the clear, frosty sunshine. When they
reached the coasting-ground, it looked absolutely perfect; and a score of sleds, with twice as many boys,
were already at work upon it. The sliding-down that
slope was something to wonder at; but the climbing
back again was another thing altogether. It was
easy enough for Vosh, however, to make a bargain
with one of his boy-friends to do his extra driving
for him, and have the cutter ready for use every
time, with, of course, just a little waiting.

"How often they do slip down!" exclaimed Susie,
after a long look at the climbers in the road.

"Some of 'em'll be good and lame to-morrow," said
Corry. "I don't believe you girls'd ever get up the
hill again, once you got down."

It had been thoughtful of Vosh to look out for that; but he had had some experience on that slope in other winters, and knew what he was about.

They were on the very upper level now. Vosh helped the girls out of the cutter, and at once started it off, telling the driver, —

"Go right on into Benton: that's where we're coming."

The "pair of bobs" had been the running-gear of a small wood-sleigh built for one horse to pull around among the woods. It was light but strong, and the box on the rear half of it was well supplied with blankets. When the girls were in it, and the gay red spread from the cutter was thrown in front of them, the ripper put on quite a holiday appearance.

"Susie," said Pen, "it's awful. We're going to go."

Susie made no reply; but she was conscious of a great flutter of excitement, as she nestled back upon her seat, and looked out upon the great glittering expanse of white that spread out below and beyond, until it seemed to break in pieces among the streets and houses of Benton.

There was one moment a little before starting when she almost felt like backing out.

"Port," she said, "hadn't you better come in here with us?"

"Yes, Port," said Vosh, "get in. There's plenty of room. We'll be all the better for more weight."

Port was glad enough to accept, and he knew every other boy in sight was envying him. There had been no end of comments on "Vosh Stebbins's ripper."

It was curious, but hardly any fellow who had a sled of his own had, at the same time, any faith that "them bobs'll steer."

Away went Corry the next instant, on his swift little hand-sled, darting down over the slippery crust like a sort of — well, like a flash of boy.

"Shall we go through the village?" asked Susie, with a half-shuddering idea that when they were once a-going they would never stop.

"See about it," said Vosh. "We'll make the longest trip ever was run down this hill."

"We're going, Susie!" exclaimed Pen. "Hold your breath. We're going."

They were starting, sure enough, and Susie felt that she was turning a little pale; but they moved slowly at first, for the slope was very gentle there.

"Vosh, does it steer?" said Pen.

That was the very thing he was experimenting on; and the other boys did not guess why the new contrivance made so many curves and turns as it did, until he was able to shout, —

"She works! See? I can twist her in any direction."

"I'm so glad!" exclaimed Susie.

"Now, girls!"

The ripper made a sudden dash forward, down a steeper incline, faster, faster. And there was no need to tell the young-lady passengers to hold their breaths: that seemed the most natural thing in all the world to do.

There never was a more slippery crust, and the ripper almost seemed to know it.

Faster, faster, shooting down the steep slopes, and spinning across the level reaches; and all the while there was Vosh Stebbins bracing himself firmly, as he clung to the long arms of his rudder.

It was well he could guide so perfectly, for the gaps in the fences were none too wide, after all; and if he and his cargo should happen to miss one of these, and be dashed against a fence — It was altogether too dreadful to think of, and there was no time to think of it.

The cargo had great confidence in their "engineer and pilot," as Port had called him before starting, and they had more after they shot through the first gap.

The wind whistled by their ears. The country on either side was but a streak of white. Nobody could guess how fast they were going now.

"There's the village!" gasped Port.

"The river!" whispered Pen.

"O Vosh!" began Susie, as they shot into what she saw was a road lined with streaks of houses and fences.

Before she could think of another word, they were out on the ice of the little stream, and a skilful twist of the rudder sent them down it instead of across. In a moment more they were slipping smoothly along over the wind-swept surface of the frozen mill-pond; and the ripper had lost so much of its impetus, that there was no difficulty in bringing it to a standstill.

"There!" said Vosh, as he held out his hand to help Susie alight, "that's the longest slide down hill anybody ever took in Benton Valley. Nobody'll beat that in a hurry."

"I don't think they will," she said; and Pen added inquiringly, —

"We ain't scared a bit, Vosh. We'd just as lief have another."

That was what the sorrel colt was coming down the road for; and they were speedily on their way up, more envied than ever.

"Don't I wish aunt Judith was here now!" exclaimed Pen.

"She'd never ride down hill in this thing," said Vosh. "I'm glad she didn't see us come."

There was a great deal of work before the sorrel colt that morning, and knot after knot of curious spectators came out of the village "to see how Vosh

Stebbins had gone to work and beaten that there Cobbleville ripper."

"He's a cute one."

"Regular built genius."

"There ain't such another feller in Cobbleville. He beat 'em all at spellin', too."

Vosh had won fame as well as fun, and all Benton was proud of him. For all that, he was tired enough by dinner-time, and was glad to drive his passengers back to the farmhouse.

"Aunt Judith," said Susie, "it was splendid! You never saw any thing like it! Wonderful!"

There was a great deal more to be told, and it was all true; but it was not easy for aunt Judith and Mrs. Farnham to believe it.

"Do you mean to tell me that that thing didn't stop till you were out in the middle of the mill-pond?" asked aunt Judith; and four young people with one voice told her it was nearer the upper end than the middle.

"Well," said she, "I s'pose it must have been so, but there was never any such sliding down hill before up this way. I'd like to see it done just once; that is, if it didn't just happen, and can't be done again, nohow."

CHAPTER X.

THE DEER-HUNT ON THE CRUST.

THAT Saturday afternoon was a quiet one at the farmhouse. It really seemed as if there had been excitement enough for one day. Still, as aunt Judith was in the habit of remarking, —

"Sometimes you can't always tell for sure what's a-coming."

Vosh Stebbins came over after supper, and he met Deacon Farnham at the gate. There was nothing unaccountable in that; but the boys heard him say, just as he was following the deacon in, —

"No, we won't need any snow-shoes. I'll take mine along."

"I'll take mine too, but the crust's strong enough without 'em."

"It'll be weak in spots in the woods: Sile Hathaway says it is."

Those were great words for two boys to hear, — "woods" and "Sile Hathaway."

"Port," said Corry, "something's coming."

"Hark!"

"Yes, deacon, Sile says the deer break right through, every here and there. There's droves of 'em, and the storm's kind o' driven 'em down this way."

"I've known it happen so more'n once."

"Port," whispered Corry, as if it were an awful secret, "I know now: it's a deer-hunt on the crust."

"Oh-h!" was all the answer; and in half a minute more Vosh was on the stoop with them. Then he was in the house. Then the whole affair burst out like a sudden storm.

Deacon Farnham did not say much; but there was a flush on his face, and a light in his eyes, that made him look ten years younger. Mrs. Farnham told him so. But Pen interrupted Vosh halfway in the explanation he was giving Susie, by exclaiming, —

"O mother! may I go?"

"My child" —

"I never saw a live deer killed on the snow. If Susie goes, may I go? — Are you going?"

Susie could hardly help saying, —

"I know I can't go, but I'd like to."

"Port!" exclaimed Corry, "let's get out the guns, and clean 'em. It won't do to have 'em miss fire."

"That's a good idea," said his father. "Vosh and

I'll want to set out early Monday morning. You won't have time to clean 'em before you go to school."

"School! Monday!"

"Now, Joshaway," exclaimed aunt Judith, "don't tease the boy that way. He won't miss just one day's schoolin', and the crust ain't going to last forever. If Mrs. Stebbins can spare Vosh" —

"My mother? Why, she'd go herself if she could."

"Well, Corry," said his father, "if you and Port'll agree not to kill too many deer, you may go."

Port was still wrestling with the painful idea of a gun missing fire after it was actually pointed at large game. There was something dreadful and incredible about it; and, when the weapons were brought out, he cleaned away at them almost painfully.

Deacon Farnham attended to his own rifle. Then he took a ladle, and melted some lead at the kitchen fire, and moulded a score or so of bullets.

"Will that be enough?" asked Port.

"With those in my pouch? I'd say they would. If I get a chance to use half a dozen, I'll be satisfied. You boys'd better take plenty of buckshot, though. You'll be sowing the woods with 'em."

Susie did not exactly care to handle those "shooting-irons," as Vosh called them; but there was a strange fascination about them, after all. She could understand why, when they were all laid down on the table, aunt Judith put on her spectacles, and came and peered at them all over, and said, —

"They ain't much like the guns we had when I was a girl. They used to kill heaps o' game, too."

"What is the difference, aunt Judith?" asked Susie.

"Well, 'pears like these ain't much more'n half as big and heavy. Double bar'ls, too, and all our'n was single. We had flint locks, and didn't know what percussion-caps was. 'Pears to me, if I was goin' a-huntin', I'd ruther have one of the old kind."

Pen counted her father's bullets over and over, till she could hardly tell whether he had two dozen or four; and Corry had to stop her nicking them with the scissors.

"That's to show they're counted."

"Yes; but they won't go straight with nicks in 'em. You'll make father miss his deer."

Vosh went home early; but it was all arranged before he left the house, and it was safe to say that nobody he left behind him would go to sleep right away.

It was very hard indeed, all day Sunday, for the youngsters to keep good, and not to say more than once an hour, —

"It's good and cold. The crust'll be all right to-morrow."

The Monday morning breakfast was eaten before daylight, and it was hardly over before they heard Vosh and Mrs. Stebbins at the door.

They came right in, of course; and the first words were from her, —

"Now, Judith, you and Sarah ain't goin', are ye? I'd go in a minute, if I had a gun, and was sure it wouldn't go off. — Susie, are you and Pen goin'? I do hope there'll be deer enough for all four on 'em, and they won't come back and have to say they left 'em in the woods."

There was not much time to talk, so ready was every thing and every body; but it did seem to Port as if Vosh Stebbins's hand-sled, long as it was, was a small provision for bringing home all the deer they were to kill.

"The lunch-basket and the snow-shoes half fill it now."

"It'll do," said Vosh. "You'll see."

"Why don't you put on your snow-shoes?"

"The ice-pegs I've put in all your boot-heels'll be worth a good deal more, if the crust's what it's likely to be."

It was not a great while before they all discovered what good things to prevent slipping were a few iron peg-heads sticking out of the heels of your boots. As for the snow-shoes, nobody ever wants to wear such clumsy affairs unless it is necessary.

Old Ponto had been in a fever ever since the boys began to clean the guns Saturday evening; but Vosh had secured for that day's work the services of a very different kind of dog, — one, moreover, that seemed to know him, and to be disposed to obey his orders, but that paid small attention to the advances of any other person.

"Is Jack a deer-hound?" asked Port.

"Not quite," said Vosh. "He's only a half-breed; but he's run down a good many deer, knows all about it."

He was a tall, strong, long-legged animal, with lop-ears and a sulky face; but there was much more "hunter" in his appearance than in that of old Ponto. His conduct was also more business-like; for it was not until Ponto had slid all the way to the bottom of several deep hollows, that he learned the wisdom of plodding along with the rest, instead of searching the woods for rabbits.

"Rabbits!" The very mention of those little animals made the boys look at each other as if asking, —

"Did you ever hunt any thing as small as a rabbit?"

The snow in the woods was deep, but it was not drifted much; and the crust was hard, except close to the trunks of the trees, and under the heavier pines and hemlocks. Walking was easy, and they pushed right on through the forest.

"How'll we ever find our way back again?" asked Port.

"Follow our own tracks," said Corry. "Besides, father and Vosh'd never dream of getting lost around here. Guess I wouldn't, either."

Port looked back at the trail they had made. He thought he could follow that. Still he would have been more sure of himself in the streets of a city, with names and numbers on all the lamp-posts at the corners.

"Keep your tempers, boys. It's hunter's luck, you know. We may not get a single shot."

The words were hardly out of the deacon's mouth, before Jack sprang suddenly forward, anxiously followed by Ponto.

"He's scented!" exclaimed Vosh. "There isn't much wind; but it's blowing this way, what there is."

"Hark! Hear him?"

That was music. It seemed as if a thrill went over every nerve among them, at the cry of the excited hound, as he fully caught the scent, and "opened on it."

"There'll be a run now, Vosh."

"Not up the mountain."

"No, we won't follow yet. If they turn him, he'll come this way."

"Or down the hollow."

"No lake for him now."

"He can run on this crust."

"Yes, but he can't pick his own course with the dogs behind him."

Comments followed thick and fast, as the eager sportsmen pushed onward. It seemed to the boys a good time to do some running, if they could but know in what direction to go; but Vosh and the deacon were carefully studying what they called "the lay of the land."

Ahead of them, they knew, was a bold, steep mountain, such as no deer would climb. Half a mile to the right was the road to Mink Lake; and to the left and behind them the woods were open, with a fair amount of "running-room."

"If they turn him," said Vosh, "he'll have to pass in sight. You may get a shot, deacon. It'll be a long one, but I'd be ready if I was you."

It turned out that way in less than five minutes; for a fine doe came springing across the snow, well ahead of the dogs, and out of "shot-gun range."

"Try her, deacon! There, she's broken through! Try her!"

The deacon's rifle was already at his shoulder, and, just as the beautiful animal scrambled out upon the crust, the sharp "crack" rang through the forest.

"Struck!" shouted Vosh as the doe gave a great spring; but she dashed right onward, followed by the dogs.

"Now, boys, you run while I load."

Port and Corry hardly needed orders; and the main wonder was, that they did not break their necks in the desperate burst they made after that wounded deer. Even Jack could not do his best running over that icy crust, except when travelling in a straight line. He could not turn quickly without slipping; and the doe must have known it, to judge by the manner in which she dodged among the trees.

"Here she comes, right past us!"

Bang! went one barrel of Vosh Stebbins's gun.

"Missed, I declare! Must be I've got the buck-ague."

Bang! from Corry, and he seemed to have done no better; but just then the deer broke through at the foot of a hemlock, and Porter Hudson had what was almost as sure as a "sitting shot."

He made the best of it by letting drive with right and left. It was a long range, and the shot scattered, of course; but they afterwards found the marks of nine of them in the skin of that doe.

In twenty seconds Jack had her by the throat; and Ponto tried to imitate him, but concluded that he had better lie down and pant a little.

Vosh was on hand now, to take off Jack, and to finish the work with his long, sharp hunting-knife. He knew exactly what to do; and, when Deacon Farnham came up, they hung their game to the lower limb of a tree.

"No wolves around," said Vosh; "but it'll be safe from any kind of varmint."

"What does he mean, Corry?"

"Why, the wolves are pretty well killed off; but there are wildcats, and some other things, I hardly know what. All the bears are treed. We'll stop for our game on our way home."

They were now barely two miles from the farm-house, and they went fully another before they saw any more game. Off, then, went the dogs; and the boys were taken a little by surprise when the deacon said, —

"Vosh, you and the boys sit right down here. — No, Corry, you and Port walk off to the right there, about thirty or forty rods. I'll strike to the left as far as the edge of the big ravine. If they've really started a deer, he may come along there."

Away he went, and away went the boys. Porter Hudson had hardly been able to speak ever since he fired at the doe. It was true that his uncle had hit it first; but then, he had killed it, and he was thinking what a thing that would be to tell his city friends after he should get home. He did not know a boy among them who had ever fired a gun at a deer. Now he himself was to be that very boy, and it was almost too much. He was beginning to half dream about it, when he heard the warning cry of Jack, coming nearer and nearer, ahead of him.

Almost at the same moment he heard the crack of his uncle's rifle. He saw Corry spring to his feet, and stand still, while Vosh Stebbins darted away to the left, as if he thought he might be needed there.

"What can it be? I don't see a single thing. No — yes — there he goes, straight for Corry! Why doesn't Vosh stop?"

The deer in sight was a fine buck, with antlers which afterward proved him to be three years old; and it was easier for Corry to hit him "on the run" than to hit a white rabbit. He fired both barrels too, and he shouted to Port; but there was no more glory for the city boy this time. Corry had aimed too well, and the buck had been too near; and it was hardly necessary for the dogs to pull down their game.

"Corry, hear that? It's Vosh's gun. What's the matter?"

"There goes his second barrel. Run: your gun's loaded."

It was all in a minute; and Port darted away with a strong impression that something strange had happened.

Corry must have thought so too, for he loaded his gun like lightning.

Something strange had indeed happened.

Deacon Farnham had walked on rapidly towards the deep ravine, after leaving the boys. He had known that forest ever since he was a boy, and had killed more than one deer in that vicinity. He did not go any great distance, keeping his eyes sharply about him, when he suddenly stopped short, and raised his rifle.

It looked as if he were aiming at a clump of sumach-bushes; and Port, or even Corry, would probably have said they saw nothing there. Vosh, perhaps, or any hunter of more experience, would have said, —

"See his antlers, just above the thick bush? See 'em move? He's gazing now. He'll be off in a jiffy."

If left alone, but not so fast after the deacon had fired; for, after he had seen those antlers, he could guess pretty well at the body below them. He could not correctly guess its exact position, however; and so, instead of hitting the deer in the chest or side, the bullet grazed his shoulder, and struck his right hip. There was no more "run" after that in that magnificent buck, but there was plenty of fight. There was danger, too, in his sharp and branching horns, as Deacon Farnham discovered when he so rashly plunged in among those bushes.

Danger from a deer!

Exactly. Danger of being gored by those natural weapons of his.

Instead of being able to use his hunting-knife,

the deacon found himself dodging actively behind trees, and fending off with his empty rifle the furious charges of his desperate assailant, until Vosh came to his assistance.

It was a very good thing that Vosh came when he did, and that his gun was loaded. Two charges of buckshot were fired at very short range; and the deacon was safe, but he was pretty nearly out of breath.

"You were just in time, Vosh."

"Glad I was. Isn't he a whopper? Sile Hathaway was right. The deer haven't run as well, down this way, since I remember."

Port came running up just then; and he was all eyes and ears, although his help was not needed.

"He's a grand one! We've got another."

"Have you?" panted his uncle. "Vosh, you go and 'tend to it. I'll 'tend to this one soon as I get my breath. Guess we've got all the game we want for one day."

"Why, uncle, it isn't much after noon: we might kill some more."

"Well, we might, but it'll be late enough when we get home. We've work before us, Port. Time we had some lunch, anyway."

They were all ready enough for that; but the boys began to discover soon afterwards that deer-hunting was not all play. It was easy enough to cut down branches of trees, and lay them on the sled, and fasten them together. Then it was not a terrible lift for all four of them to raise a dead deer, and lay him on the branches.

The tug of war came afterwards, as they hauled that sled homeward over the crust. Several times it broke through; and then there was no end of floundering in the snow, and tugging and lifting, before they again got it a-going. Then once it got away from them, and slid away down a deep, steep hollow, landing its cargo all in a heap at the bottom. There was no use for the snow-shoes, but they had to be fished for in the snow when the sled broke through.

It was a long pull, but they all worked at it until at last they hauled the sled out into the half-made road to Mink Lake. After that, they got on better; but they were a weary lot of hunters when they reached the farmhouse, and the day was about gone.

There were eager faces at the windows, that of Mrs. Stebbins among them. There were shrill shouts from Pen on the front stoop. Then there was an excited little gathering at the kitchen-door, when the sled was drawn in front of it, and the deacon exclaimed, —

"There! Look at 'em!"

"Three of 'em!" exclaimed aunt Judith. "All real good ones, too. Now, when I was a girl, I've

known the men folks go out and bring in six of a
morning, and they didn't have to go more'n a mile
from the house."

Mrs. Farnham was equally well satisfied, and Pen
clapped her little hands in a gale of excitement.

"Poor things!" said Susie.

She could hardly help feeling a little sorry for
those three beautiful creatures on the sled; but Mrs.
Stebbins curtly remarked, —

"Nonsense, my dear: they was made to be killed
and eaten. — Deacon, did you and the boys kill any
on 'em?"

She had a vague idea that the glory of that hunt
must somehow have been won by "my Vosh;" but
Susie had just time to say, —

"They look so innocent, so helpless!" when her
uncle exclaimed, —

"Innocent! Helpless! That big buck was within an inch of making an end of me when Vosh came
up and shot him. — He's your game, Mrs. Stebbins."

He forgot to mention that the fight with the buck
was all his own fault, for he began it; but the story
helped Susie out of her bit of soft-heartedness, and
it made Mrs. Stebbins hold her head up amazingly.

"O father!" said Pen. "Did he hurt you? He's
a dreadful deer."

"I think, Pen," said her father, "I'll let you eat
some of him for supper."

There was venison-steak in abundance at table, and Corry was nearly justified in declaring, —

"It's good fun to hunt deer, but I'd rather eat 'em than drag 'em home."

CHAPTER XI.

ON THE ICE.

BOTH Vosh Stebbins and Corry Farnham had a great deal to do in their hours before and after school. The former, particularly, had chores upon his hands which would have been a great burden to a less thoroughly efficient and industrious young fellow. He had his sorrel colt, instead of the two teams and the oxen of the other farm, and he also had cows and pigs. As to these and the poultry, Mrs. Stebbins relieved him of much, for she said of herself, —

"I'm as spry as a gal, and I don't show no signs of failin'. I don't intend to hev that boy choked off from havin' his sheer of all the goin's-on he can reach out to."

She was a notable housekeeper and manager, and was free to say so. As for Corry, not a little of the work put upon him was what his father wisely called "farm-schooling;" but he had it to do, just the same.

162

One consequence was, that the splendid skating prepared by the thaw and rain and freeze on the mill-pond had not received the attention it so well deserved. Some of the village boys had done what they could for it; and it lay there waiting for the rest, just as good as ever. Porter Hudson had looked at it longingly more than once; and it was only the day after the grand deer-hunt on the crust that he said to Susie, —

"Now, don't you say a word about it to any one. Put your skates under your shawl, and walk on down to the village with me. I'll wrap up mine in a bundle."

"What if anybody should see us? Who cares? I don't."

"Why, Susie, don't you see? We'll be out with all the rest before long. We haven't been on our skates since we were at the rink last winter. I don't feel more'n half sure I could stand up on mine."

"No, nor I: that's a fact. We must have some practice first, or they'll think we're just learning."

They felt very wise about it, but they had no notion whatever that precisely such an idea had occurred to Vosh Stebbins. His mother had not minded his getting home pretty late on the two or three evenings when she knew he was educating his feet and ankles before showing Susie Hudson and her brother what a country boy could do on good ice.

"Your father," she said to him, "was the best skater in the valley, and you ort to be. Get your skates filed, Lavawjer." And she told him a great deal about ice and skating before she felt satisfied that he knew what might some day be required of him as being her son and the smartest boy in Benton Valley.

So it came to pass, the day after the hunt, while Penelope and her brother and Vosh and all the other boys and girls were safely shut up in the village schoolhouse, the boy and girl from the city were out upon the ice. They even took pains to keep at the upper end of the pond and on the river above it, so that not one critical pair of eyes should discover what they were about. It was a complete success, as far as secrecy was concerned, and nearly so in other respects. The first trial could not be too long, but it compelled Port to remark when they set out for home, —

"How stiff and lame I am!"

"Port," replied Susie, "I can't but just walk."

"We must try it again right off," said Port, "or it won't do. If we can manage it to get down there two or three times more" —

"Without any one seeing us" —

"We can skate as well as we ever could: shouldn't wonder if it surprised 'em."

Vosh had had a sort of surprise in his own mind, and he had worked it up among the other boys. It came out only a few evenings later, when aunt Judith was compelled to exclaim at the supper-table, —

"Skating-party on the ice! Who ever heard tell of such a thing! After dark too!"

"Yes, ma'am," said Corry gravely: "the skating's to be done on the ice, — all over it. There'll be the biggest bonfires you ever saw, and there'll be good moonlight too."

"Sakes alive! — Susie, would you like to go and look on for a while?"

"Indeed I would! Now, aunt Judith, you and aunt Sarah both go, and take Pen and me."

There was a little discussion of the matter, of course; but the deacon settled it.

"I used to think there wasn't any thing much better'n a skate by moonlight. It won't pay to hitch up a team, but I'll walk over with you. Let's all go."

The first whisper Port gave to Susie after supper was, —

"Hide your skates. I'll let 'em see mine: they don't know I can stand on 'em."

Corry was right about the moon, and the evening was wonderfully clear and bright.

"Plenty of light to skate by," said the deacon

when they started; but even he had to admit that
the village boys had done themselves credit, when
he reached the pond, and saw the bonfires.

There must have been nearly a dozen of them
strung along from the dam to the mouth of the little
river on both shores; and one big one flared up right
in the middle of the pond.

"It'll melt through," said Pen.

"Guess not," replied her brother. "The ice is
awful thick."

There were a good many merry skaters already at
work; and there were groups of spectators here and
there, for the fires made the scene well worth coming
to look at.

"Susie," said Vosh, "how I do wish you knew
how to skate!"

"Let me see how you can do it. I'll look on a
little while."

She felt almost conscience-smitten about her intended fun; but she kept her secret until all the
boys had strapped on their skates, and she heard
Vosh say to Port, —

"Can you get up alone? Shall I help you?"

"No, I guess not. Can you cut a figure 8, this
way? Come on, Vosh, catch me if you can!"

"Corry!" exclaimed Pen, "Port can skate. See
him go!"

"I declare!" remarked the deacon, "so he can."

"So can Vosh," said Mrs. Stebbins. "There ain't any city boy going to beat him right away."

Vosh's effort to find out if that were true had already carried him so far away, that, the moment Corry followed him, Susie felt safe to say, —

"Now, uncle Joshua, if you will help me buckle my skates "—

She was in such a fever to get them on, that she hardly heard the storm of remarks from Mrs. Stebbins and aunt Judith; but the deacon seemed to take an understanding interest in the matter, and he was right down on his knees on the ice, hurrying to fasten those skates for her.

"Can you really skate, Susie?"

"I'll show you in a minute. Please do hurry, before either of them suspect any thing."

"O Susie!" said Pen mournfully, "I do wish I could."

"You must learn some day."

"Susie!" exclaimed aunt Judith, "wait for somebody to go with ye: you might tumble down."

"Start, now, Susie," said her uncle. "Off with you!"

She was really a very graceful skater; and her aunts looked on with admiration, as well as a vast deal of astonishment, while she made a few whirls near by, to make sure her skates were on rightly. Then away she glided over the ice; and the first

thing Vosh Stebbins knew of it was when the form
of a young lady fluttered swiftly past him, between
him and the glare of the great central bonfire. Her
face was turned the other way, and his first exclama-
tion was, —

"What a splendid skater! Who can she be?"

"I know," said Port Hudson, close at hand, and
waiting for his share of the joke. "She's a girl from
the city, and she's spending the winter with some
relatives of mine. Come on: I'm going after her.
Think you can keep up? Come on, Vosh."

Away went Porter, just as his friend felt a great
hot flush come into his face, and dashed after them,
exclaiming, —

"If I ain't stupid! Why, it's Susie Hudson herself!"

He felt as if his honor were at stake, and he had
never skated so in all his life before. The fires on
the bank seemed to flit by him as he followed that
solitary girl-skater around the glittering icy reaches
of the mill-pond. It looked so like a race, that almost
everybody else paused to watch, and some even
cheered. Deacon Farnham himself shouted, —

"Hurrah for Susie!" and Pen danced up and
down.

"It's jest wonderful," said aunt Judith, "to see
her go off that way the very first time."

"Guess it isn't quite the first skatin' she ever

did," said Mrs. Stebbins; "but Vosh'll ketch her, now, you see'f he don't."

Susie had somehow got it into her head that she did not mean to be caught, and her practice was all in her favor; but just as she reached the head of the pond, and made a quick turn into the winding channel of the river, Vosh came swinging along at her side, and for a little distance he did not speak a word to her.

"Vosh," she said, after trying very hard to think of something else to say, "I wish you'd teach me to skate."

A ringing laugh was all his answer for a moment, and then he remarked innocently, —

"The ice is smoother up this way, but I mustn't let you get too far from the folks. Tire you all out skating back again."

On they went, while all the people they had left behind them, except their own, were inquiring of each other who the young lady could be that had so astonished them.

Oddly enough, the Benton girls had omitted skating from their list of accomplishments, by a kind of common consent; and Susie's bit of fun had a surprise in it for others besides Vosh and her aunts. It was quite likely she would have imitators thereafter, but she had made an unexpected sensation that evening.

Even Port had surprised Corry and the Benton
boys, although some of them were every way his
equals on the ice.

"Now, Vosh," remarked Susie at the end of nearly
a mile of that crooked ice-path, "we'd better go back.
Are you tired?"

"Tired! I could skate all night. We'd better
go, though, or aunt Judith'll borrow a pair, and
come skating along after us."

Down the river they went again, and across the
pond; and by that time a score of busy tongues were
circulating the discovery.

"It's that there city cousin of the Farnhams.
She learned how to skate when she was travellin' in
Russia."

Part of that news may have had some help from
Corry; but Susie's aunts were glad to get her back
again, and Mrs. Stebbins said to her, —

"You never did look prettier nor nicer. I do jest
like to see any gal nowadays that ain't afraid of her
shadder."

"Guess Susie isn't much afraid of any thing," said
Pen; "but I'm awful glad there wasn't any holes in
the ice."

"No air-holes are needed on a mill-pond," said Mr.
Farnham; "but, if I'm not mistaken, there'll be some
lame young people to-morrow. Nobody feels very
well the day after such a race as that."

He was not altogether wrong. Susie felt pretty well the next day, but in spite of her practising beforehand, her race with Vosh Stebbins had been a severe one ; and, to tell the full truth, he himself was willing to get over the effects of it before volunteering to try another.

CHAPTER XII.

A VERY EXCITING WINTER EVENING.

The people of Benton valley and village had not been ignorant of the fact that Deacon Joshua Farnham's family had some city cousins spending the winter with them. Some had said at first that they were there for their health, and some that they were orphans and had come to stay; but the facts of the case got around after a while.

Susie and Port had made some acquaintances at the donation, and some at the spelling-match, and some at the meeting-house; but people had not exactly made up their minds what to do about them. Now came the altogether sensational affair of the moonlight skating-race on the mill-pond, and something had got to be done.

Away over on the other side of the valley, and just in the outer edge of the village, stood a great white, square box of a house, larger than any other house within ten miles of it. Squire King was by all odds the richest man in that circumference, and he had built his house large accordingly. Mrs. King was not exactly proud, although she knew she was rich, and that she had been to Europe once, and to a number of notable places in the United States. Neither she, nor any other woman in or about Benton, was in a position to look down upon the Farnhams. She liked them, as did everybody else, and was a little in awe of aunt Judith; but she had not felt any social duty in the matter of their visitors until she was told of the skating. It had really been pretty well done on the ice, but it was tenfold more wonderful when it was described in Mrs. King's dining-room. Even Squire King himself dropped his newspaper, and listened, and asked, "What's the world coming to?" And Mrs. King's three lady neighbors who were telling her about it were unable to answer him. They all said, however, that it was time some special attention should be paid, and that such a young lady must be worth getting acquainted with. So had said every girl in the valley who felt old enough to skate; and quite a number of well-grown boys decided to learn new "curly q's" on the ice. Every boy of them had a bump on the back of his head within three days, and the pond was less like a looking-glass than formerly; but Mrs. Squire King had made up her own mind in less time than that, without any headache. There should be a young people's party at her house; and her husband agreed with her, that the nearer they could fill it up, and leave standing-room, the better.

"Do it right away, Addie," said he. "Do it right up to the handle. Kind of startle folks. Nobody's a-looking for any such thing to come."

It was to be all sorts of a surprise; and the whole valley went about its affairs, just the same as if Mrs. Squire King were not manufacturing so much frosted cake, and boiling tongues and hams for sandwiches. Some other tongues would have been hot enough if they had known a word about it before the invitations were written and sent out.

Up at Deacon Farnham's it was a little quieter than it was anywhere else the day after the skating, until he himself came in from the village at noon. He had come for his dinner, but there was a look in his face as if he had bróught something. Pen had seen it there before; and she asked him what it was to be, precisely as if he had spoken about it.

"What have I got? How do you know I've got any thing?"

"Is it something for me?"

"No, not this time, Pen; but I've something for Port and Susie."

"Letters, uncle!" exclaimed Susie; and Mrs. Farnham added, —

"I do hope so. She's been fairly mourning for some, day after day."

"It's all a mistake or neglect of somebody in your father's office in the city, Susie. There's three for you, and one is a fat one. Where's Port? There's as many for him."

Port was out at the barn; but Pen found him, and brought him in, as if his life depended upon getting those letters at once.

"Mother! Father!" said Susie, with a face that changed fast from red to pale, and back again, as she dropped into aunt Judith's big rocking-chair, and began to read those letters.

"Is it all good news?" asked Mrs. Farnham in a minute or so.

"All perfect, aunt Sarah. Mother seems to be doing very well."

She read on and on; and Port had now come in, and was doing the same; and it was as if with one voice they suddenly exclaimed, —

"How strange it seems!"

"What is so strange?" asked aunt Judith in almost a tone of alarm. "Did any thing happen to either of 'em?"

"Happen! No, indeed, but it's warm weather there. Father complains of the heat. Green grass and trees, and flowers and birds, and no sign of winter! Seems as if it couldn't be in the same world."

"I don't half believe I'd like that kind of winter weather, anyhow," said aunt Judith with emphasis.

"When it's time for snow, I want snow, and plenty of it. 'Pears like to me, it would be kind of unnatural without sleighin'. Now, this here winter's been the most satisfactory we've had for four years past. It's been a real genuine, old-fashioned, right down cold and snowy winter."

" And it's getting colder now," said Deacon Farnham. "There's no telling where the thermometer'll go to, if it keeps on trying."

Nevertheless there was a curiously pleasant feeling to be had in listening to those accounts of the different condition of things in Florida; and Port was justified in remarking, —

" I'd like a little of that balmy air for a while in the morning, but I wouldn't care so much for it after I once got well a-going."

" I would," said Pen. " I could go a-sleighing, and keep my feet warm all the while."

" Shouldn't wonder if people down there would like a little of our ice at this very time," said her father; while Susie herself declared, that, except for seeing her mother and father, she did not wish to exchange winters with them.

When Corry came home in the afternoon, the first thing he said was, that he was glad Pen had returned at the midday "letting-out."

" The wind blows down the hill with an edge like a knife, and they say it's away below zero,"

"It's coldest at the foot of the hill," said Pen confidently; and then, while Corry was warming himself, Susie and Port read to him tantalizing things about orange-groves and magnolia-trees and sunshine, and boat-rides on the St. John's River, away down in the sunny South.

"That's where De Soto hunted for the Fountain of Youth," said Corry; "and I guess Eden must have been around there somewhere. It wasn't down in Benton Valley, anyhow you can fix it."

"Nonsense!" said aunt Judith. "You'd get sick of any kind of Eden that didn't need a fireplace for six months in the year."

Corry's ears were beginning to feel better, and his opinion of the weather he was accustomed to improved as the tingling subsided. Still he was quite willing to discuss a little more fully the wonder of tropical and semi-tropical lands. Even after chores were attended to, and supper was eaten, and the whole family gathered in the sitting-room, they all seemed to feel more like talking than any thing else. Of course the knitting went on as usual, and Pen asserted that her next undertaking in yarn was to be a pair of stockings for Porter Hudson. It seemed as if they had just got fairly settled, before the front-gate opened with a great frosty creak, as if it pained the hinges to be swung upon in such cold weather, and the sound of a well-known voice came faintly to the door.

"If it isn't Mrs. Stebbins!" exclaimed Pen; and her mother said, —

"Glad she's come. It isn't far, but it's neighborly for her to look in on such a night as this."

"Hope Vosh is with her," said Corry as he stepped towards the door; and so he was. But they both had come upon something more than a mere neighborly call. Hardly was Mrs. Stebbins inside of the door, before she exclaimed sharply, —

"Joshaway Farnham, it's a wolf, I know it is! I heard it twice; and, if I don't know a wolf when he howls, it's because the whole country wasn't full on 'em when I was a gal. I've known a man that a'most made his livin' off the bounty they sot on wolf-skelps, till they found out that he was raisin' of 'em at a place he had away back under Sawbuck Mountain; and they paid as much for pups' ears as they did for growed-up wolves, and"—

"Angeline Stebbins!" almost shouted aunt Judith, "what do you mean? There hasn't been a wolf down so far as this, these three years and more; and then they never came nigh any house except Josiah Rogers's hog-pen."

"Fact, though, now, I guess," said Vosh. "I listened hard, and I believe I heard one howl."

"Shouldn't wonder at all," said Mr. Farnham; "what between the deep snow, and the hard, cold snap. It isn't so much because they can't run down the deer so well, I believe, as because they somehow get bolder, and sort of crazy, in bitter frost. Did you hear more than one, Vosh?"

"Can't say, unless the same one howled several times. I heard it first when I was out at the barn, and it sounded just in the edge of the woods."

"I don't believe one could get at your stock very easily, or at mine. You don't feel like a tramp out after wolves on such a night as this?"

"My gun's leaning against the door outside," said Vosh, "if you care to come along. Mother said she'd rather stay here till I got back."

"No more chance of killing one than there is of flying," remarked Mrs. Farnham; "but if Joshaway wants to go" —

The deacon's pleasant blue eyes had been kindling a little under their shaggy brows; and he was now slowly rising from his chair, and buttoning up his coat.

"I'll go as far as the woods with you, Vosh, and see what's the matter. — We won't be gone a great while, Sarah. I'll only take my double-barrel: a rifle's of no use by moonlight. Where are Port and Corry?"

Nobody had seen them slip away; but their chairs had been empty from the moment when they heard the word "wolf," and saw Vosh Stebbins's shot-pouch slung over his shoulder. The deacon had hardly picked up his overcoat, before they were in the room again, loaded with guns and shot-pouches.

"Going for wolves, are you?" said the deacon. "You won't kill any. Not one has been killed this side of Sawbuck Mountain for years and years. Come along. Wrap your ears up, and put an extra slug into each barrel on top of the buckshot."

Rifle-bullets answered capitally well for slugs, and even Pen and Susie felt a tingling all over when they saw those guns loaded. Ponto was called in from the kitchen; and he too seemed to be all tingle, as soon as he saw the hunt-like look of matters.

"He couldn't whip a wolf," said Corry, "but he might be of some kind of use."

"My father had a dog once," began Mrs. Stebbins; but she was interrupted by aunt Judith with,—

"Now, Angeline, you sit right down, and we'll have up some krullers and some cider; and they'll all be frosted back again in time to eat their share of 'em."

Ponto was doomed to disappointment that time; for Mr. Farnham, on second thought, fastened him up in the kitchen again, remarking, —

"He'd only spoil any other chance we might have. — Come on, boys. Judith is pretty nearly correct about the weather, and I guess I'm right about the wolves."

"I heard 'em," said Mrs. Stebbins; "but they

didn't say they'd sit down under a tree and wait till you came along."

They were hurrying out of the door as she said that, and there was no danger of their walking slowly. They had not reached the gate, before Mr. Farnham straightened up, exclaiming, —

"I declare! Hark!"

It was neither so faint nor so far away that they could not hear it; and it might have been the howl of a lost dog, for all that Porter Hudson would have known. There was a hurrying up the road, after that; and the frost was all but forgotten in the excitement of getting to the woods as soon as possible. There was hardly any talking done; and the snow of the road broke with a brittle, cracking sound under their feet.

"There it is again!" said Vosh at last, as they drew near the shadows of the forest; "and it sounds as if it were nearer."

"Nearer it is," said the deacon, "and so is something else. I'd like to know, now, just how many miles they've been chasing that deer. Hear him jump?"

His ears were better trained than those of his young companions, for he had all his life been a keen sportsman; but, on listening attentively, they all declared, one after another, that they could hear something. Again they heard the voices that were coming nearer, but they were more like yelps than howls this time; and Mr. Farnham at once asserted, —

"They are gaining on him. He has turned again, and is coming this way: shouldn't wonder if they'd been after him all day. Hold still, boys: better chance out in the open."

Yelp, yelp, jump, jump! and the hunters were shivering with cold and excitement, for they knew not how many or how few minutes more; and then, out through the frosty trees, in his last desperate race for life, dashed an all but tired-out buck. He had run well and far, but he had reached the limit of his strength. He hardly noticed the four hunters, in his fear of the enemies behind him. Not one of them thought of lifting a gun at him; but, just as a staggering leap carried him down from a snowdrift into the road, he slipped and fell. A few seconds earlier, Vosh had hoarsely whispered, —

"There they come, — pair of 'em!" And two long, dark forms, that seemed to glide on in a series of silent undulations, were only a few rods behind the buck.

"They'll get him," said Port, with a keen sense that his blood was warming suddenly.

"Father!" exclaimed Corry, "you say when."

Before the buck could regain his feet, his fierce pursuers were upon him with savage snarls, and his race for life was over. There was a vivid picture of forest-life for one tremendous moment, there in the middle of the road; but within thirty yards were the four sportsmen, and their guns were at their shoulders.

"Keep your second barrels for a moment," said the deacon. "Be sure of your aim. Now!"

The four reports followed one another in swift succession, and a storm of slugs and buckshot was hurled into the struggling group in the road. The buck was down already, but he rolled clean over now. One wolf lay kicking on the snow beside him, while the other gave a bound and a yelp that told of a shot reaching him.

"Take that one, all of you! the other's done for. Quick!"

The deacon fired as he spoke, and the rest followed so fast that nobody could even so much as guess who killed that wolf.

Down he went, and the sudden hunt was all over. Two wolves had run down a deer, only to deliver their own peltry with it to the astonished sportsmen they had summoned by their ill-advised howling.

Porter Hudson could hardly believe his ears and eyes. He had heard of wonderful hunting, and now he had actually done some on his own account. There were the forest savages dead in the road; and there was Deacon Farnham finishing up the deer, and saying, —

"We couldn't have done that if Ponto had been here: he'd have rushed forward, and been in the way of our shooting. We'd have lost both of them."

"We've got 'em now," said Vosh.

"One skin's yours, and half of the buck," said the deacon; "and now we'd better go for your colt and a sled, and haul 'em home."

That was bitter cold work, but nobody seemed to care where zero was just then. The sled was brought and loaded, and then it was drawn to the very kitchen-door of the Farnham farmhouse.

Ponto's nose had told him something, and he was barking furiously at the other side of that door. Lights were hurrying into the kitchen, and the door sprang nervously open.

"Joshaway, what's this? Was anybody hurt? We heard the firing," gasped Mrs. Farnham in a tone of intense anxiety.

"Oh, it's awful!" began Pen, but aunt Judith was calmer.

"Got a buck, did ye? It wasn't that that did the howling."

"Sakes alive!" shouted Mrs. Stebbins. "That's a wolf! I knew Vosh would kill something. Two on 'em? Two wolves and a deer? And you wasn't gone no time at all; but Sarah and Judith, they said it seemed as if you was going to stay all night. — Pen, don't you tetch 'em. — Susie, what do you think of that ? — Joshaway Farnham, don't you ever tell me again that I don't know the kind of howl a wolf makes."

There she paused for a moment, and the hunters had a chance to tell how that very remarkable affair had actually come to pass.

"Just so," said aunt Judith. "It was the buck tolled 'em down for ye. They'd never have dreamed of coming, frost or no frost, if they hadn't been a-follerin' of that deer."

She was entirely correct, but it was pretty late that night before all was quiet in either of those two farmhouses. The game was slung up to the rafters of the woodshed, to be more thoroughly attended to in the morning. The excitement could not be slung up anywhere, and Susie Hudson was aware of a grisly feeling that the country was hardly as safe a place as she had been in the habit of thinking. She was very glad, however, that there were guns in the house, and she all but wished that she knew how to load and fire one.

CHAPTER XIII.

A FIRESIDE STORY.

PORTER HUDSON had a great deal upon his hands the forenoon following the coming of those wolves. He had to see his uncle take off their skins and that of the buck; and he had a great many questions to ask about wild animals in general, and wolves in particular. Pen had informed him, before she went to school, that the two wolf-skins were to be turned into buffalo-robes for Vosh's cutter and her father's big sleigh. She may also have been correct when she added, "They're the best kind of blankets you can get." Susie herself took an interest in that, for she was already crocheting the most fanciful red border she could think of for the rich fur of the wildcat they had brought home from Mink Lake. It promised to be an uncommonly brilliant lamp-mat.

As for Vosh and Corry and Pen, they were even eager to get to school early. The people of Benton Valley would know nothing about the wolves until the story should be set a-going. All three of them told it well, not only after they reached the school-house, but to some acquaintances whom they met on the way. If Pen's version was hardly as correct as the other two, there was certainly more of it; but her improvements were as nothing to those it received afterwards. Every boy and girl that heard it carried it home in a different shape. As many as could do so at noon were especially happy on that account; and such as lived too far away, and had brought luncheons with them, got along as well as they could, holding in, and hoping that they would still be the first to tell it to their folks.

Some were sure to be disappointed, for such news travels fast. One farmer who was in the village with a load of oats never waited to dicker about the price he sold them at, but got away at once, and stopped at six houses before he reached his own. By supper-time there were elderly ladies in the village who felt like bracing their front-gates with boards, and wondered if the wolves were really going to pester the village all winter. Perhaps the best and most vivid account of the fight was given by one small boy to Elder Keyser and his wife to carry home to Cobbleville. His description was very good, of how the buck led the wolves into Deacon Farnham's kitchen; and how Mrs. Farnham and aunt Judith and Mrs. Stebbins, and Susie Hudson and

Pen, were there all alone, eating apples, till the men came in from hunting, and helped them. The elder had a meeting to go to that evening, or he would have driven over at once to inquire into the matter, and see if any of the family were really very badly bitten by those ferocious wild beasts. He took "Wolves in sheep's clothing" as a text for his next sermon, and it was most attentively listened to. Elder Evans and his wife got out their horse and cutter at once, and went in a hurry: so did Mrs. Squire King, only she took her big double sleigh, with the longest gilded goose-necks in that whole region. There were six ladies in it by the time she reached the foot of the hill below the Farnham homestead; for she was a good neighbor, and loved company. Somebody was out looking at the wolf-skins until nearly tea-time; but not one soul would stay to tea, after obtaining all the facts of that affair to go home with.

All that Mrs. Squire King saw of Susie Hudson made her feel more in earnest about the party; but she resolutely sealed her lips over it, except in a small bit of confidential talk with aunt Judith and Mrs. Farnham, and the five ladies who went with her in her own sleigh to see about the wolves.

It was a very busy tea-table, for ever so many people had to be talked about, and what they said had to be repeated; and Pen broke down entirely in trying to rehearse a wolf-story the teacher had told the scholars who staid in at noon. It turned out to have been a tiger-story with an elephant in it, and Pen had added the snow on her own responsibility.

After tea a little while, Vosh came over with a sled to get his wolf-skin and his share of the buck; and it would have been a small miracle if his mother had not come with him. The weather was every bit as cold as it had been the night before, and she said so as she entered the house.

"Never mind, Angeline," said aunt Judith. "Sit right down, and take off your things, and there won't be any howling done to-night."

"I jest do hope not, Judith Farnham, for I waked up nine times afore mornin' last night, and each time I was kind o' dreaming that I heard something; and it kep' me every now and then, all day, a-remembering that story of old Mrs. Lucas and Alvin Lucas, and that was ever so long ago. And it always did seem to me one of the queerest things; and you can't account for it, nohow."

"What was it, Mrs. Stebbins?" asked Susie. "Couldn't you tell us the story?"

They were all sitting around the fireplace; and Susie was gazing at a flickering blaze on the top log, or she might have noticed that her uncle and aunts had not said a word.

"Tell it? Well, I s'pose I can; but it isn't much

of a story, after all. They do say that story-tellin's
a good thing of a winter evening, when it's as cold
as this ; but I wasn't ever much of a hand at it, and
it's got to be an old story now, what there is of it."

Vosh had no doubt heard the story, and knew what
was coming ; but both Corry and Pen joined with Port
and Susie to urge Mrs. Stebbins a little. The deacon was still silent, and aunt Judith and Mrs. Farnham seemed to be knitting more rapidly than usual.
Mrs. Stebbins hemmed twice to clear her throat, and
drank some cider, and said it was a good thing to
know how to keep it sweet all winter by putting in
a chunk of lime while it was a-fermenting ; and then
she told her story.

"There's a wolf in it," said Pen to Porter Hudson ;
but it went right along, just the same.

"The Lucases they owned the farm we live on
now ; and it's a right good one, as soon as Vosh is
old enough to handle it himself. That was away back
when your uncle Joshaway was a young man, and he
and Alvin Lucas were the closest kind of friends ;
and there wasn't a likelier young man around here
than Alvin was, unless it was Vosh's father or your
uncle Joshaway. It was before either one of 'em was
married ; and the war broke out the spring before,
and it seemed as if all the young men was half crazy
before harvestin' was over. There was eighteen of
the very best and pick went right out from Benton

Valley, and twice as many more from over Cobbleville way, first thing, as soon as the grain was in, and some of the after-ploughin' was done. It was queer, but somehow, when they came together, they elected Alvin Lucas captain of that company; and a young fellow from Cobbleville was next; and Levi Stebbins was only a corporal at first; and your uncle Joshaway was a private, but he got to be a major before the war was over; and Vosh's father he came home a captain, with a big scar on his right arm, and he'd lost one of his front teeth in a scrimmage. But I must go right on to the wolf part."

"O Mrs. Stebbins!" exclaimed Pen with a long breath, "I'd forgot all about the war."

"So has most people," said Mrs. Stebbins; "and it's well they have, for it's only a root of bitterness now, and it ort not to be dug up for ever and ever. But that first winter after the war begun was an awful cold one, up hereaway. Leastwise, there kem a bitter snap, like the one we're having now; and somehow it seemed as if we never missed all those young men so much, not even in the fall work, as we did after winter sot in. There was a good many fireplaces like this all over the country, where the folks missed the best face they had, for the one that isn't there always kind o' seems to be the best; and old Mrs. Lucas she counted on Alvin, most likely, a good deal as I do on Vosh. He was away down on the

Potomac with his company, and there hadn't been a man of 'em hurt up to the time of that cold snap, and they sent letters home as reg'lar as clock-work ; and people thought the war wasn't sech a dreadful thing, after all, so long as nobody got killed from Benton Valley and Cobbleville. Your folks lived right here, and mine away over on the other hill, nigh the dividing-line into the Sanders school-district ; and your grandfather and grandmother Farnham were alive, and Susie Farnham she hadn't married Reuben Hudson and gone to the city, and Judith she was a young woman ; and those two gals was at home with the old folks one evening "—

Just then Deacon Farnham got up from his chair, and sat down again ; and aunt Judith rubbed her spectacles very hard indeed, and Mrs. Farnham looked at her, sidling, as if to see if she were interested in the story ; and Pen looked around at every one, for she knew that Mrs. Stebbins must be getting pretty near the wolf now.

"It was one bitter cold night, and all the Lucases were at home, except, of course, Alvin; and there were four younger than he was ; but he was the likeliest, as well as the oldest, and his next brother didn't go into the war till the second year. Old Mrs. Lucas wasn't nervous generally, but that night there seemed to be something the matter with her ; and it was as dark as a pocket, as well as being so cold you could hardly keep the hens from freezing. She kept a-going to the window; and her husband, I heard him tell my mother about it, how she seemed to be listening for something, and all of a sudden she broke out, 'John, it's a wolf! Hear him! He's out there in the road! Something's happened to Alvin!' Now, I ain't a mite superstitious, and she wasn't, and John Lucas wasn't; but there was a charge of buckshot in his gun, and he took it up, and went right out " —

"Was the wolf there ?" asked Pen with widely open eyes; for Mrs. Stebbins paused a moment, as if for breath, and aunt Judith's knitting had dropped into her lap, and she was staring hard at the fire.

"Yes, Pen," went on Mrs. Stebbins, "and he was nigher the house, and he howled again; and he sot still, and held his head up to howl, till John Lucas and his next son — Roger, his name was — got within shot of him; for he was crazed with the frost, jest as wolves will get in sech times."

"Did they kill him ?" asked Corry.

"Dead as a mackerel," said Mrs. Stebbins. "And he was the biggest kind; but it didn't seem to comfort Mrs. Lucas a mite, and it was the strangest kind of a thing, after all. There isn't any superstition in me : but, when the next letters kem from the war, there'd been a scrimmage on the Potomac that very night; and Capt. Alvin Lucas, and four men from Benton Valley, and twice as many from Cobbleville, had been killed in it."

"I don't believe the wolf knew a word about the skirmish," said Port. "He couldn't, you know."

"Besides," said Pen, "they shot him; and he couldn't go all around the valley, and over to Cobbleville, and howl for the other folks."

Susie was just going to say something to aunt Sarah about it; but she and aunt Judith had suddenly arisen, and were walking out into the kitchen. Mrs. Stebbins looked down at her knitting, just the same, and finished her story as she toed out the last half-inch of that stocking.

"It kem awful hard on John Lucas, and he sold out his farm that next spring, and went West; and Levi Stebbins bought it as soon as his army time was ended, and he could come home again; and Joshaway he staid in till it was all over. Old Mrs. Lucas, it took her awful; but she was a good woman, for she said she couldn't get her mind right about losing Alvin till she could feel to sympathize with the mothers of men that was killed on the other side. I never had no trouble about that, for Levi he always spoke well of the Southern soldiers, and so did your uncle Joshaway; and mothers are mothers, no matter where you find 'em."

Mrs. Stebbins was quiet for a moment, and then remarked, —

"Lavawjer, it's time we was a-going home."

"I guess it is, mother."

It was while she was getting on her things that Deacon Farnham beckoned Susie Hudson away into the parlor entry for a moment, and whispered to her, —

"You are old enough to know some things, Susie. Don't say any thing more about that story. Speak to Port, and I will to Corry. Your aunt Sarah's elder brother was the first man killed in that skirmish: that was what came to her."

"And aunt Judith?"

"Capt. Lucas. They were engaged."

"O uncle Joshua!"

"That is what the war meant to both sides, my dear."

"I'm glad it was ever so long ago, and we don't know any thing about it," said Susie; and that was about what Port said when they spoke to him. It was not much of a wolf-story, after all, but it had helped away a winter evening, and perhaps it had done something more; for the boys and girls of one generation should not be ignorant, altogether, of the sufferings and sacrifices of those who have lived and died before they came to take their turn at it.

CHAPTER XIV.

THE BEAR-TRAP.

WHEN the family came down to breakfast the next morning, it looked as if every thing but the venison-steaks and johnnycake and hot coffee had been forgotten. The steaks were capital; and as for the johnnycake, nobody in all Benton Valley could beat aunt Judith at that sort of thing. She was proud of her skill, and liked to see its products eaten; but even as Porter Hudson was helping himself to his third slice, she said to him, —

"Once, when I was a girl, I remember being out of bread for a whole week."

"O aunt Judith!" exclaimed Pen, "didn't you eat any thing?"

"We had plenty of milk and pork and eggs and poultry, and we didn't starve. We pounded corn in a mortar and made samp, and we hulled some corn and made hominy, and ate it, and did capitally well."

"I think I could live a while on such starvation as

that," remarked Susie, "especially if I had maple-sugar to melt down, and pour on the samp."

"We had some," said aunt Judith; "but we were just about out of flour and meal, when there came a thaw and a freshet; and the mill-dams all gave way, as if they'd agreed to go down together; and we had to wait till the mills got to running again. It wasn't easy to get a grist ground, even then; but we didn't suffer any. Folks sent ever so far for flour; but there wasn't any railroad then, and the roads were awful for a few weeks. There used to be great freshets in those days."

"That's a thing that might come any time after the bears turn over," said Mr. Farnham; and Port instantly asked him, —

"After the bears turn over! What have they to do with it?"

"Didn't you know that? Well, well! You're a city boy, and don't have any bears at home. Every bear hunts up a hollow tree as soon as it's too cold for him to get around in the woods comfortably, and sits down before it till there's a heavy snow. Then he creeps in, and gets the hole snowed up, and goes to sleep. He never dreams of waking up till spring; but, as soon as the sun is hot enough to warm the tree on one side, it makes him comfortable on that side of him, and he turns over in his sleep to warm the other. It's a sure sign of a thaw; and the snow melts pretty fast after that, till it's time for him to creep out and get something to eat."

"How hungry he must be!" said Pen.

"When is the best time to hunt for bears?" asked Port, with a dim idea that he would like to boast of having killed a few.

"Along in the fall, when the nuts are coming down. They're fattest then. They trap 'em every year all through the mountain country north."

"Trap 'em! Is there any trap big enough to catch a bear in?" asked Port.

"Big enough! I'd say so. And sometimes it's a wolf, or a wildcat, or a panther, instead of a bear; and I know of a man getting caught in one once."

"Did he get out?" asked Pen.

"I won't tell you about it now; but when we get into the sitting-room this evening, I'll let you know just how one man made a bear of himself away up on Sawbuck Mountain."

That was something to look forward to; but not long after Corry and Pen had gone to school, Porter Hudson took his gun, and marched away to the woods, all alone by himself. The crust was still as firm as ever, and there had been no snow worth mentioning since the great storm.

"I don't know exactly what I'm going to kill," he said to himself; "but I'm ready for any thing that comes."

His first call for Ponto had been obeyed somewhat fatly and sluggishly ; but, the moment the old dog saw the gun, he was another and a more willing animal. He led the way, head and tail up, until he came to the spot in the road where the wolves had pulled down the buck. The new snow, thin as it was, covered all traces of that adventure. But Ponto's memory, or nose, made him precisely accurate. Port was quite willing to stop a moment, and recall how that spot had looked in the moonlight, and how uncommonly loud and sharp had seemed to be the reports of the guns. All the hills had echoed them ; and it occurred to him, that, if he should now meet a pack of wolves, he would have but two loads of buckshot, instead of eight.

"And no slugs," he added. "I should have brought some along. I don't care, though. I could climb a small tree, and fire away."

He afterwards noted quite a number of small trees well adapted to such business. So were some lower limbs of several larger trees, and he stood for a few minutes under one of these. He imagined himself sitting on that great projecting branch, climbing out to where it was ten feet above the snow, with a large pack of very ferocious and hungry wolves raging around below him, while he loaded and fired until the last of them had keeled over.

"Wolves can't climb," he remarked to himself ;

and he felt that such an affair would be grand to tell
of when he should get back to the city. It would
make a sort of hero of him, and the wolves could be
skinned right there. He enjoyed it mentally; but
that particular pack of wild beasts, killed off, in his
imagination, under that tree, were all the game, of
any kind, that he obtained that day. Ponto did
better, for he discovered innumerable tracks in the
snow, and they seemed to answer his purposes admi-
rably. He could sniff and bark, and run and come
back again, and look up into Port's face as if he were
saying, "There, I've had another hunt."

Port had one. In fact, he hunted until he was
sick of it, and decided that it was altogether too cold
to hunt any longer. It seemed to him that he had
been gone from the house a very long time indeed;
and he was all but astonished, on his return, to discover that he was quite in season for dinner.

"Didn't you see any thing whatever?" asked
Susie. She had felt a little anxiety about him, considering what dreadful things the forest was known
to contain, and was even relieved to have him
reply, —

"Not so much as one rabbit. You never heard
any thing so still as the woods are."

"Didn't know but what you might bring home a
few deer," said Deacon Farnham, "or find a bear-
tree."

"I'm good and hungry, anyhow," said Port; "and it's the hardest kind of work, looking all around for nothing."

He had not done that. No city boy can spend a morning in the winter forest, with a gun and a dog, without learning something. It is an experience he will not forget so long as he lives.

Those had been great days for Vosh Stebbins. He felt that he had new duties on his hands ever since his new neighbors came, and was more and more inclined to hurry home from school in the afternoon, and get his chores done early. His mother remarked more than once that she had hardly one moment to say a word to him, and that he could split more wood in half an hour than any other boy in Benton Valley. Nevertheless it was at their own supper-table that evening that she said to him, —

"We'd best not go over to the other house to-night, Lavawjer. We've been there a good deal lately, and I like to be neighborly, and it's a good idee to help 'em with their city cousins, and I never seen any that I took to more'n I do to Port and Susie Hudson; but there's reason in all things, and we mustn't be runnin' in too often."

Vosh buttered another hot biscuit, and did not make any reply, because he could not think of the right one to make. It was made for him just a little

after tea, when he told his mother that every thing
he had to do was done. She had cleared away the
tea things, and had taken her knitting, and both of
them were sitting by their own fireplace.

"Our sittin'-room," she said, "isn't as big as
Joshaway Farnham's, and it doesn't call for more'n
half so much fire; but it's a nice one, and I wish we
had more folks into it. We must ask 'em all to come
over some evening, and I'll see if I can't make 'em
feel comfortable. I'll make some cake, and we've
got a'most every thing else on hand. And that
makes me think: I want Judith Farnham's new recipe
for makin' the kind of cake she had Christmas and
New-Year's; and you can put on your overcoat and
come right over with me, and we won't stay one
minute, and you mustn't let them get ye to talkin'
about any thing." And Vosh was beginning to get
ready before she reached that point. She put away
her knitting at once, and said there was plenty of
wood on the fire, for they were coming right back;
and so Vosh piled on two more large logs, and they
started. He may have had ideas of his own as to
how much wood might burn while he and his mother
were walking to Deacon Farnham's and returning.
Some short walks are long ones, if the people who
walk them are not careful.

"I'm real glad they've come," said Mrs. Farnham
the moment she heard her neighbors at the gate.

"They're good company, too, and it must sometimes be kind of lonely for 'em, — only two in the house, and no young people."

Her fireside had no lonely look, and it was all the brighter for those who now came in. It was of no manner of use for Mrs. Stebbins to speak about cake, and say she had not come to stay. Vosh settled himself at once with a hammer and a flat-iron and some hickory-nuts; and aunt Judith pulled up a rocking-chair, remarking, —

"Now, Angeline, don't let us have any nonsense. Sit right down here and be comfortable. I'll make a copy of the receipt for you to-morrow, and I always put in more eggs than it calls for."

"Vosh," said Pen, "you mustn't make too much noise. Father's going to tell a story. It's of a man that got lost in the woods, and made a bear of himself."

"I've known fellows do that, and not go far into the woods either," said Vosh; and Susie thought a moment before she added, —

"So have I. But then, some men can be bears, and not half try."

The deacon laughed, and put down the apple he was paring.

"I don't know if it's much of a story," said he; "but it has one advantage over some other stories, for it's a true one. — Take an apple, Mrs. Stebbins.

—Corry, pass them to Vosh.—Pen, well, keep the cat in your lap if you want her."

"Now," said aunt Judith, "I guess everybody's ready."

"I won't go home till after the story, nohow," said Mrs. Stebbins; "but speaking of bears" —

"Mother," interrupted Vosh, "you've dropped your yarn. Here it is."

"Hem!" said the deacon. "There were more bears all around the country once than there are now, and they did more mischief. It was really worth while to take a hunt for 'em now and then; and there's always a good market for bear-skins, if you cure 'em well. The way my story came about was this : —

"There was one November when the woods were just full of deer, and some young fellows from Benton Valley made up their minds they'd have a good hunt before the real cold weather came. There hadn't been just such an Indian summer for years and years, and camping out in the mountains was no kind of hardship. The nights were cold, but the days were warm; and all four of them were strapping young men, used to taking care of themselves, and brimful of fun.

"They went up beyond Mink Lake, and it looked as if the deer kept away from them all that first day. They'd have gone to bed hungry, if it hadn't been

for some fish they caught; and the next morning
they made up their minds they'd go out singly, in
different directions, and see which of them would do
best. What was curious, they didn't have but one
dog along, and his owner counted on having the most
game, as a matter of course."

"He was the man that got beared," whispered Pen
to the cat in her lap; but her father went right on, —

"The man that owned the dog started out from
camp right along the slope of Sawbuck Mountain,
northerly; and there are little lakes every mile or so,
and they're just swarming with fish. He was following an old path that was pretty well marked.
Maybe it was an old Indian trail; but white men
had followed it in winter, for the trees were blazed,
so you could follow it if there was snow on the
ground to hide it."

The deacon paused a moment, as if thinking how
to go on; and Porter Hudson asked him eagerly, —

"Did he have the kind of luck I had yesterday?"

"Well, not exactly," replied his uncle. "Before
it was ten o'clock by his watch, he had killed and
hung up three deer. Real fat ones they were, too,
and one of them was a seven-year-old buck with
horns that were worth having."

"'Pears to me," remarked Mrs. Stebbins, "the
deer nowadays don't have the horns they did when
I was a gal;" but the deacon went right on, —

"He didn't know just how many miles he might be from camp; and he knew he'd need help in carrying in those deer, unless he should cut up the meat and set out to smoke it right there."

"And good smoked deer-meat is something worth having," said his wife.

"But he walked on for half a mile or so, just as if there was any use in going for another deer that day, till he came out into a sort of open. The land sloped down to the shore of a little lake as regularly and smoothly as if it had been cleared for a deer-pasture. There wasn't a deer on it just then; but right in the edge of the opening the hunter found something that set him a-thinking. It was a little the best bear-trap he had ever seen. There was a ledge of rocks; and about the middle of it was a break that made a square place the size of a small bedroom, only it wasn't much more than six feet high by ten feet deep. The fellows that made the trap had built up the front with heavy upright logs to hang their gate on, and covered the top with logs."

"Please, uncle Joshua," said Susie, "what is the gate for?"

"To let the bears in. Did you ever see a figure 4 rat-trap? That's it. The gate lifts up, with a strong sapling for a hinge, and the ends of the sapling (that's the roller) are fitted into the logs at the sides. There's a long pole fitted into the gate to lift it by, and, when that's pulled down flat on top of the trap, the gate is up about level. There was a wooden catch geared through the roof of that trap so nicely, that, when the pole was in the notch of it, the trap was set to spring at any kind of pull on the bait. The lower end of that catch hung away back by the rock, and the whole machine was in prime order."

"It was somebody else's trap," remarked Corry doubtfully.

"Oh, he could see that nobody had been there that year. The timber was all seasoned, and there was grass growing against the gate. There was a good stiff latch, made with a deep notch in the logs to hold that gate after it came down; and, if a bear once shut himself in, there was no possibility of his getting out. The hunter looked it all over, and made up his mind he'd set the trap, and go back to the last deer he'd killed, and get some fresh meat for bait, and see if something could be done with it. It was some time before he could get at the pole so as to bring it down; but he worked it with a grape-vine for a rope, and it came into place perfectly. Then he went to his deer, and got his bait, and hurried back, as if he were afraid some beast or other would get caught before the bait was there to account for it. You use it just as you use toasted cheese in a rat-trap, only you tie it on, so it'll take a hard pull to get it off. A bear is sure to pull, and that springs the trap; a panther isn't so apt to be stupid about it; and a wolf won't, unless he's hungry. They're more cunning than a bear is, anyhow."

" He didn't toast the whole deer, and put him on?" said Pen.

" No, he didn't toast any thing; but he was hard at work, tying all he had taken from the inside of that deer to the catch of the trap, when something happened that he hadn't been looking for."

" Was it a bear?" said Pen.

" Worse than that. He had pulled too hard on the catch, and it had slipped the pole free, and down came the gate with a bang, and he had trapped himself completely. The gate just missed the dog when it fell, but it left him outside. The first thing the hunter did was to laugh. Then he said he would finish tying the meat on, and go up and set the trap over again. He tied it on carefully, and set out to get ready for bears; but, when he tried to lift that gate, it wouldn't lift. It was made heavy purposely; and it was caught in the notch below, just exactly right, for the man that made that trap knew how. There was nothing about it to laugh at, and the hunter sat down and thought it over: so did the dog, looking at him through the cracks of the logs, and whimpering. It doesn't take a good dog long to understand when things are going badly."

" He could have chopped his way out," said Port.

"Yes," said the deacon, "but he had no axe, and a jack-knife is a poor tool to work with on seasoned timber. He tried it for a while ; but it seemed as if he might whittle away for a week, or till he starved to death, before he could make a hole to get out by. He couldn't dig under, for limestone rock is hard digging. He worked a little at the roof, but that had been weighted with heavy stones, so that a bear could not have stirred a log of it. On the whole, it was a pretty tight place to be in ; and it was dinner-time, and he was tremendously hungry. He had not a mouthful to eat or drink, and he knew his friends would not be uneasy about him before night, and not much even then. He was uneasy already, and so was the dog. The poor fellow came and pawed at the logs, and whined and whined ; then he went back, and stood and barked like mad at the whole concern."

" What a pity he didn't have an axe to chop himself out !" said Pen. " Then he wouldn't have staid there and starved to death."

" He didn't do that exactly," said the deacon. " He sat down and thought about it, and studied that gate, until by and by an idea came to him. It was the middle of the afternoon before it came, but it was a good one. There were splinters of wood around the floor of the trap, and he had whittled a heap of shavings from the log he had worked on. He gathered them all, and began to crowd them into the chinks of the logs, away up in both corners of the gate, just under the roller that it swung on. Soon as he'd got them well packed in, he took out his match-box, and set them on fire. There isn't any trouble about getting dry wood to burn; and it was plain enough, that, if the ends of that roller were burned away, the gate would have to go down."

Everybody around that fireplace felt sure about the burning qualities of seasoned wood, for they all had to pull away a little, and the story went on.

"The fire kindled well on both corners. The fact was, it kindled a little too well, and it spread, and the smoke began to come back into the trap. Just before the hunter took out his match-box, he had looked around for his dog, and the fellow wasn't any-where to be seen. There was time now to wonder what had become of him, but no amount of whistling brought him. Then the smoke grew too thick to whistle in, and the hunter lay down to get some fresher air at the bottom of the gate. The fire spread to the logs of the roof, and began to climb down the gate, and the trap became the hottest kind of a place. It took a long time for all that; but there was plenty of excitement in watching it, and in wondering whether or not he was going to roast himself to death instead of getting out. It grew hotter and hotter, until it could hardly be endured, and the smoke was stifling. At last the hunter sprang up, and gave a shove at the gate with all his might. If he had done it before, it might have let him out sooner. The gate went over upon the ground with a crash, and one jump carried the man out of the trap. He had left his rifle outside, leaning against a tree; and there it was yet, but there was not a sign of the dog.

"He had left a big piece of deer-meat out there too; and his next thought was that he had plenty of fire to cook by, and that he wanted some supper as soon as he had been to the lake for a long drink of water. That water tasted good, now, I tell you, and so did the broiled meat afterwards; for the sun was only an hour high, and he had had an early breakfast that morning. He sat and cooked and ate, and felt better; and all the while the fire was finishing up the bear-trap, roof and all. He did his cooking on the gate; and, if he had not been able to get out when he did, the gate and roof would have cooked him."

"Oh!" exclaimed Pen. "And he wasn't hurt a mite?"

"No," said her father; "and just as he finished eating, and rose to pick up his rifle and start for the camp, there came a yelp, yelp, yelp through the woods, and there was his dog got back again. He hadn't come alone either; for right along behind him, travelling good and fast, were the three other hunters. The dog had been to the camp for them, and made them understand that his master was in trouble."

"Splendid!" exclaimed Susie.

"And when they saw the smoke of that fire, they all shouted and ran, till the dog gave a howl and a jump, and began to dance around the man he belonged to. He told his friends the whole story, and there was the fire to prove the truth of it; and each of them had killed a deer that day."

"And how did you ever come to know just exactly how it all happened," said Mrs. Stebbins, "so't you can tell it right along, 'most as if you'd been there?"

"Well," said the deacon, "I suppose it's because I was the man that got caught in the trap; and the other three were Alvin Lucas, and Levi Stebbins, and Sarah's brother, Marvin Trowbridge, that's living now at Ticonderoga."

"I'd heard the story before," said aunt Sarah, "and I remember seeing that dog when he was so old he was gray."

"I guess he didn't get turned out of the house when he was old," said Port enthusiastically; "but why didn't you fix the trap, and set it again?"

"That's the very thing we did; and we caught three bears in it, and one wildcat, before the snow came. Only we always took care to bait the hook before we set the trap; and nobody else had to set it on fire to get out of it."

"Vosh," said his mother, "as soon as I've finished this apple, it'll be time for you and me to be getting ready to go home."

"That's all," said the deacon.

•

CHAPTER XV.

THE NEW CHESSMEN.

PORTER HUDSON did nôt feel like going to the woods the following morning. He had a pretty clear idea that they were empty, that the bears were asleep in their trees, that the wolves had mostly been killed, that the deer had run away, and that the cougars and wildcats had gone after them. He was quite willing to go to the village with Susie, when she told him she must go and see if she could find some tidy-yarn, and some more colored wool for the last few inches of the fringe for the fur of the Mink-lake trophy.

"There's three stores," said aunt Judith, "and you'll be sure to find what you want at one of 'em. I can remember when old Mr. McGinniss kept the only store in Benton, and it did seem sometimes as if he never had nothing in it that you wanted to buy. It was always something else that he'd picked up at a bargain, and was asking two prices for, and it didn't make him rich neither."

214

The walking in the road was good enough now, and from the very outskirts of the village the paths were all that could be asked for; but Port looked at them several times with remarks about Broadway.

"If we were there now," he said, "we'd find all the flagging clear and clean of snow."

"I almost wish I could be there for an hour or so," replied Susie. "There'd be a better chance of finding just what I want than there is here."

The stores of Benton Village, however improved they were since aunt Judith was a girl, bore no resemblance whatever to those of the great city. There was a cheese on the counter over which Susie first asked for colored wool; and the young man she spoke to took down a large pasteboard box of crewel and other stuff, and politely carried it to the front window. He set it down on a pile of home-made sausages, and lifted a bag of flour out of her way, so that she could make a search. She found one skein that would do, and only one, and she bought it.

"Now, Port, we will try the next. I've made a beginning."

"That's more than I thought you would do," said he. "It's a mixed-up sort of place."

So was store No. 2, but it had a long showcase for that description of goods, and for fishing-tackle and candies, and for a lot of stuff that looked as if it might have been intended for Christmas presents to the heathen.

"It must have been some accident," said Susie almost as soon as she looked into that collection. "Here are the very things. We needn't go any farther."

The merchant, who was smiling across the show-case at her, knew that she was "that young lady from the city that's visiting with Deacon Farnham's folks, and she can skate like a bird."

He had never seen a bird skate, but he knew she was pretty, and he was sincerely proud of the fact that she found the right wool in his establishment. He was doing it up satisfactorily, when Port pointed at a box in the showcase, and asked, —

"What's that, Mr. Rosenstein?"

"Dot is chessmen. I show you."

The box was lifted out in a twinkling, and pulled open.

"I thought as much," said Port.

They had evidently been on hand a long time, and had a forlorn and forsaken look. The white king was in two pieces, and so was one of the black horse-men; but Mr. Rosenstein said encouragingly, —

"I zell dose chessmen for two shilling. Dey cost me four. You joost dake a leetle glue" —

"Guess I can," said Port. "I'll buy 'em. — That's what I've been thinking of, Susie. Vosh can beat me at checkers, but he never played a game of chess in all his life. I'll show him something."

Mr. Rosenstein was again very much pleased, for that box had been a bad speculation; and Port and Susie were bowed out of the store a great deal.

There was not much to see in the village after that, but they strolled around for a little while. There were many people in from the surrounding country; and the jingle of sleigh-bells, and the continual coming and going of teams, made things lively.

One large double sleigh, with extravagant goose-necks, pulled up almost in front of them, and a lady's voice called to Susie, —

"Miss Hudson!"

"Mrs. King! Good-morning. I've been doing some shopping."

"Hope you succeeded better than I can do. Glad I've met you. There are your invitations, and your aunts' and uncle's; and if you'll be kind enough to send over Mrs. Stebbins's to her" —

"I'll attend to that with pleasure," said Port, reaching out his hand for the white envelopes her own was offering.

"And you must all come," said Mrs. King. "I'm going to have my house full. You will not disappoint me? Most of 'em will be young folks, but I'll have a few grown-up people on my own account."

Susie promised faithfully, and Mrs. King drove on.

"I'd like it first-rate," said Port, as he read his own invitation to the party. "We must go, Susie. It'll be fun."

"Of course I'll go. Don't you think she has a very pleasant face?"

He spoke strongly of Mrs. King's face, and they turned to go home. The fact that a young-people's party was getting ready to be announced at Squire King's was a secret pretty well known and carefully kept by all Benton; but everybody was glad to get an invitation, just the same. Twenty-three people, or perhaps twenty-four, remarked that they were very glad Squire King's house was so large, or there wouldn't be room in it to walk around after the folks got there. That was not all; for some of the Benton people found out, for the first time, that they were no longer considered "young people," and some of them felt as if Mrs. King had made a mistake in her reckoning. Mrs. Bunce, the doctor's wife, asked her where she drew the line; and she said, —

"I don't exactly know, but if they've got gray hair, or their children go to school" —

"That'll do," said Mrs. Bunce. "It hits me in both places. My Sam and his sisters'll be there, and I'll come after them. I hope you'll have a good time."

There was some stir at the Farnham and Stebbins homesteads over those invitations. Both houses had been swept by Mrs. King's list in order to make sure of Susie and her brother, and it came as both a triumph and a trial to Mrs. Stebbins and Vosh.

"They wear white silk neckties to parties," said she to him, "and I'll see that you hev one. They say it'll be the largest young-folks' party there ever was in Benton Valley."

Some of the young folk expecting to go were very large, truly, but not all of them; for Penelope had a special invitation. That was old Squire King's work; for he knew Pen, and he declared that he wouldn't miss hearing what she had to say about the company, and things in general.

That had been a busy day for Mrs. Stebbins, but her cake had turned out splendidly.

"They're all coming over after tea, Lavawjer," she said to him, "and we must see to it that they have a good time. If you and Porter Hudson play checkers, you needn't mind a-letting of him beat you for once. He hasn't won a game on you yet."

That was a fact; but there was something in store for Vosh that evening. He had every thing around the house attended to in prime good season; and his fireplace wore as bright a glow, for its size, as did Deacon Farnham's own. The weather called for that sort of thing; but everybody was now so accustomed and hardened to it, that there was less difficulty in understanding how the Russians can make out to be happy after their frosts begin to come.

The entire Farnham family, Ponto and all, turned

out in a procession soon after supper, and they made
a noisy walk of it to their neighbor's gate.

"There they come!" exclaimed Mrs. Stebbins;
"and they're all talking at once, and it sounds as if
they were in good sperrets, and we must keep 'em
a-going, and you mustn't talk too much yourself, and
give 'em a fair chance, and " —

The door flew open at that moment, and Pen's
voice shouted, —

"They're all a-coming, Mrs. Stebbins! — O Ponto!
I never ought to have let you get in. — Vosh, turn
him out before he has time to shake himself."

It was too late for that, and Mrs. Stebbins would
not have had a dog of the Farnham family turned
out of her house at any time. Ponto was made at
home by everybody but the cat; and even she showed
very plainly that she knew who he was, even if she
could not call him by name.

"Here we are," said aunt Judith. "Did your cake
come up? Hope it didn't fall."

"Fall! No. It's just the lightest kind. Now, do
get your things off, all of ye, and sit down. I'm to
your house often enough, and I'm right glad to hev
the whole of you in mine at once, and not scattering
along."

The room looked all the cosier for not being large;
and, as soon as everybody had found a chair, Vosh
was justified in saying to Port and Corry, —

"Now, if this isn't first-rate, I'd like to know what is."

Port's reply was, —

"I got me a set of chessmen down in the village to-day, and I brought them over with me. It's worth all the checkers."

Everybody seemed disposed to take an interest in that matter. The chessmen were turned out of their box, and showed signs of recent discipline. They had a bright and much-rubbed look. A little glue had remounted the knight, and set up the broken king; and when Corry remarked, "Didn't he get 'em cheap?" he expressed the general opinion.

Vosh looked at them eagerly, and began to set them in their places. He had never played a game of chess; but he had watched the playing of several, and that was something to a good checker-player. It was not all new ground. From the moment he had heard about Port's purchase, by way of Corry, his mind had busied itself with his memories of the games he had watched; and he was at this hour crammed full of enthusiasm for the royal game.

"Vosh," said Port, "suppose Susie and I play a game, and you look on and learn the moves."

"No," said Susie: "you and Vosh play, and I'll be his adviser. I can play as well as you can."

"Better too, if I make blunders in the opening."

"Lavawjer," remarked his mother, "that's what

you'd better do; and I don't suppose you can learn much in one evening, but you can make a start at it. They say it's an awful hard thing to get into, and there was a man over in Scoville's Corners that went crazy just a-studying over it."

The chessmen were in place by that time, and so were the players; and Susie began to explain to Vosh the different powers of the pieces. He listened politely, but it seemed to him as if he already began to see into the matter. He was only too confident of what he saw, for a trifling neglect by him of Susie's advice enabled her brother to announce what players call "the scholar's mate" in a very few moves.

"I told you so, Lavawjer," said his mother. "She knew jest what she was about, and you didn't." But there was no danger that her son would ever again be defeated by so simple a combination. The second game, with Susie's help, was more protracted; and then it was aunt Judith's keen eyes that detected the state of mind Vosh had arrived at.

"Susie," she said, "let him alone this time. He's got a-going now. Don't say one word to him, and let's see how he'll work it out."

"I won't speak, Vosh," said Susie. "Go right ahead now. — It won't be long, Port, before he'll catch up with you."

Vosh was not a conceited young fellow, but he

had a fair degree of self-confidence. He was not afraid of any reasonable undertaking at any time, but he had a queer experience coming to him just now. He found his imagination running away ahead, and placing those men on the board in new positions, and then understanding what would be the consequences of those arrangements. It was the power to do that very thing which had made him so good a checker-player; but he had never used it so vividly as now, and it almost startled him. All the brains in the world are not made upon the same pattern, and not many boys with good heads on their shoulders know what is in them.

The older people were having a good time in their own way, but every now and then they turned to watch that third game of chess. Susie was in a fever several times, and came very near breaking in with advice, as her pupil seemed running into dangers. Each time she checked herself; and each time Vosh discovered the snags ahead of him, and avoided them. Port himself was getting more deeply interested than he had expected, and called up all he had ever learned. He was not a bad player for so young a one, and he had worked out problems, and studied printed games. He remembered one of the latter now, that seemed to fit his present case very well, and he tried to make it serve as a trap for Vosh Stebbins. It seemed a success at first, but it was just like Joshua Farnham's bear-trap exactly: the fellow that was caught in it destroyed it altogether. There was a way out of the proposed defeat which had not been seen by the newspaper problem-maker, and Vosh found it.

That was the end of the game; and, in a few moves more, Port was himself in a tangle from which he could not escape. He was beaten. He was tremendously exercised by the laugh that went around the room, and by Susie's patting him on the head and advising him to wake up. He had not dreamed of any such result, and called for another trial. That game he managed to win, and one more; but beyond that neither he nor any other but a really good player was likely to go with Vosh Stebbins.

"I declare, Sarah!" exclaimed the deacon at last: "we've staid too late. We must go home at once."

Mrs. Stebbins protested that it was early; but the game of chess was over, and go they did. Every slice of all that remarkable cake had been eaten, and all declared that they had had an uncommonly pleasant evening. Pen improved it by remarking, —

"Port's had a pretty hard time, but he'll get over it."

After the company were gone, and the house was quiet, and Vosh could go to bed, it seemed to him as if he should never get to sleep. It was not exactly the fact that chess-problems were troubling his brains: it was more the yet greater fact that he had discovered brains in his head that he had not known of. With that also came the idea that he must find some better use for them than any kind of game could give him.

CHAPTER XVI.

WINTER FLOWERS AND THE PARTY.

SQUIRE KING was one of the most liberal of men, and he had something to be liberal with. He had gradually gone more and more into the spirit of the young folks' party matter, and had even astonished his wife by the things he did and proposed.

To have had actual dancing would have offended some of the best people in the village; but every other kind of amusement that was to be tolerated he provided for, and he almost doubled the allowance of ice-cream and confectionery. He had no idea, nor had even his wife, what an amount of work and of contriving they had provided for their neighbors. Every store in Benton Village, and some over in Cobbleville, did a better business from the hour in which Mrs. King's invitations were delivered.

The family at the Farnham homestead seemed to concentrate their interest upon the kind of appearance Susie Hudson was to make. Even Pen remarked to her, —

226

"They all know me, and they won't care so much how I look; but you're from the city, and every one of 'em'll look at you as soon as you come in."

Susie had brought a good enough wardrobe with her; and aunt Judith herself declared it extravagant, but at the same time selected the best things in it for use at Mrs. King's party.

"I shall have no trouble at all," said Susie. "There needn't be any thing added to that dress."

"No," said Pen, "it's mine that's got to be added to." But there was one lady in the neighborhood who was of a different opinion.

The very morning of the party, Mrs. Stebbins said to her son, —

"I don't keer if you do miss a day's schoolin'. You jest hitch up the colt after breakfast."

"Going somewhere?"

"I'll tell you after we're a-going. It won't be any short drive, now. I'm going to hev my own notions for once. She's the nicest gal I know of."

"Do you mean Susie Hudson?"

"I'll show you what I mean, and if I don't open somebody's eyes!"

She evidently had some plot or other on her mind, and she grew almost red in the face over it at the breakfast-table. She finished putting away the dishes while Vosh was out getting ready the colt and cutter, but she did not seem disposed to tell even herself precisely what her plans were. It was not until she and her deeply interested driver were actually driving into Benton that she came out with it.

"Vosh," she said, "take right down the main street, and out the Cobbleville road. We're going way to cousin Jasper's."

"That's three miles beyond. Well, it isn't much of a drive in such sleighing as this is. The colt's feeling prime. But what's it for?"

"We're going all the way to cousin Jasper Harding's; and, if the frost hasn't clean killed out his hot-house, I'm going to hev somethin' for Susie Hudson that the rest on 'em can't get a hold of. The last time I seen him he said his plants was doing first-rate, and he'd put in steam-pipe enough to save 'em if the frost was a-splitting the rocks. He hasn't any use for 'em on earth, except that he had lettuce and radishes for his Christmas dinner."

There was steady work for the sorrel colt after that, and the bells jingled the merriest kind of tune right through Cobbleville without stopping. When "cousin Jasper's" was reached, it was nothing but a long-built, story-and-a-half white house, with no pretension whatever. There were young fruit-trees around it in all directions, and uncommonly extensive trellises for vines; and at one end the glass roof of a hothouse barely lifted itself above the snow-banks. One man, at least, in that region, had materially added to his other resources for winter enjoyment.

" He says it doesn't cost him any thing to speak of," said Mrs. Stebbins to Vosh. " He's got some fixings rigged to the big stove in the parlor, to send the steam around the hot-house, and the fire doesn't go out in that stove all winter long. I'd kind o' like to try it some day myself. It's the getting started that costs money."

" And then," said Vosh, " there's the knowing how to do it."

He thought so again after he got into that bit of a winter garden, and looked around him. Cousin Jasper Harding was an under-sized man, and his wife was a short woman of twice his weight. They could stand erect where Vosh had to stoop a little; but he could stand up in the middle, and see what they pointed out to him. Both were glad to see him and his mother, and to have them stay to dinner; but, for some reason or other, Mrs. Stebbins was slow about opening her errand. Vosh wondered a little, but he waited and listened. It was at the dinner-table that she began to tell about the young folks' party to be at Mrs. King's that evening. From that she went over to Deacon Farnham's, and told about Susie Hudson, and how pretty she was, and about her skating, and all the nice evenings at the deacon's, and at last somewhat suddenly inquired, —

"Didn't you use to think a good deal of Joshaway Farnham and his wife, and Judith, and "—

"Best friends I ever had in my life."

"I was thinking, Jasper. City girls are used to having a sprig of something to wear in their dresses to a party. Now, I know it would please Joshaway and Sarah and Judith if you'd send a bit of something green, — jest a leaf or so, not to rob any of your plants. There ain't many of 'em, and cutting 'em might hurt 'em ; and where a man hasn't but a little "—

"Something green ? Guess so. There's more in that hot-house than you think there is, Angeline."

"Well, maybe there is. It looks too nice to take out any thing of what few plants you've got."

"You just finish your pie, and come along. I'll show you something you think I can't do. I'd like to do a favor for any girl of that family. Tell her I knowed her mother 'fore she was born. I'll go right in now; be ready by the time you get there. — Betsey, you keep Angeline company, and I'll show her something."

He certainly astonished both her and Vosh. As she afterwards explained to the latter, no money could have made him part with any of his hot-house treasures as a direct sale, nor would he have given them for the asking. She had to get them the way she did ; but there they were.

"That's for her throat-latch, Angeline ; and she can put that on her waistband, — little fellows, you know. She can carry that in her hand ; and, if she wants to send her photygraph to old Jasper Harding and his wife, she can. I'll hang it up in the hot-house."

Mrs. Stebbins had a great deal to say about those flowers and green leaves, and the skill with which they had been cultivated and now were put together, and she added, —

"Now, Betsey, Vosh and I must go. Jasper's bokay and the buds'll be worn by the nicest and prettiest gal at Mrs. King's party, and I wish you two were going to be there to see."

In a few minutes more the colt was brought from his dinner in the barn, Mrs. Stebbins was in the cutter guarding her prizes, the liberal florist was thanked again, and then the bells made lively music homeward.

Very complete was the astonishment on all the faces in the Farnham sitting-room when Mrs. Stebbins walked in, and announced the results of her morning's undertaking. The sorrel colt had trotted twenty miles and more for the sake of Susie Hudson ; but it was Vosh's mother who got kissed for it, and that was probably sound justice. She also received an invitation to go and come in Deacon Farnham's sleigh, and so the sorrel colt did save an evening job in cold weather.

Vosh was particularly glad of that invitation. He was a young man of a good deal of courage, but it seemed to him that he could march into Mrs. King's front parlor more easily with a crowd than with only his mother or alone. Corry was not troubled in that way, nor Penelope; and Porter Hudson was only too well aware that he was from the city, and had been to parties before. He had no doubt whatever that he would know how to do the right things in the right place, but that was just where Vosh Stebbins found his courage called for. He made a mental chessboard of Mrs. King's premises, and the people who were to be in them, and found that he could not place the pieces to suit himself. He was the worst piece in the whole lot whenever he arranged one of those society problems. It was a game he had never played, and he was only half sure he could win at it. He was confident of being as well dressed as was necessary, except that he wondered whether or not any one would wear gloves. His mother settled that for him, and Mr. Rosenstein could have told him that only three young men in Benton had bought any. These had run the risk of it, meaning to put them on if it should be necessary. One had purchased white kids, and another a black pair, while the third had heard that bright yellow was the correct thing. The pair he selected were very bright and very yellow.

Susie Hudson's dress did not trouble aunt Judith's mind after she saw it on, and she remarked of it, —

"Now, Sarah, I'm glad there isn't any thing showy about it. It's just the best thing. She isn't looking as if she was putting on. It'll be all the prettier when the flowers are there, and nobody else'll have any."

It was simple, tasteful, of very good material, and there was no question as to the good effect of the flowers. Susie was all but sorry that she was to be alone in that particular; and so, as soon as she got there, was every other girl in the room.

The deacon's hired man lived at some distance down the road, but he came up to look out for the team, and was sent first to the Stebbins house.

Vosh and his mother were ready, and he was thinking of his new white silk necktie when he came to the door with her. The man in the sleigh could not hear him think, and did not know what a burden a necktie can be; but he did hear Mrs. Stebbins remark, —

"Now, Lavawjer, the one thing you're to remember is, that you mustn't talk too much. Let other folks do the talking, and, if you keep your eyes about ye, you may learn something."

He had already begun not to talk too much, for hardly a word escaped him till they got to the Farnham gate.

"I'll go in and see if they're ready," he said, and was preparing to get out.

"I guess I'll go in too," added his mother. "I'd like to see how they're all a-looking."

At that moment, however, the front-door swung open, and a procession marched out, headed by Pen, and closed, as was the door behind it, by her father.

"We're all fixed, Vosh," said Pen. "My back hair's in two braids, and Susie's got a bracelet with a gold bug on it, and Port's got on his summer shoes, and aunt Judith" —

Just there her account of the condition of things was cut off by the general confusion of getting into the sleigh, but Pen made up for it afterwards. Vosh again showed a strong tendency to take his mother's advice, and the drive to the village was by no means a long one. They were not any too early, and had to wait for three other sleigh-loads to get out, before theirs could be drawn in front of the pathway cut through the drifts to the sidewalk. Only one of Mrs. King's guests was very late that evening, and he was a young man who was learning to play the flute, and had heard that fashionable people never went anywhere till after nine o'clock. Besides, it took him an hour or so to decide not to carry his flute with him.

It helped Vosh a great deal, that they all had to go to the dressing-rooms first, and unwrap themselves.

After that, it all came easier than he had expected, for Squire King and his wife had a hearty, kindly way of welcoming people. Perhaps it helped him somewhat, that they had no opportunity to say too much to him just then, and he could go right on following his mother's advice.

There was a stir in the rooms, that Susie did not at all understand, when she and her brother passed on to mingle with the rest of the young people. Some of them had seen her before, and some had not, and all of them were taking a deeper interest in her dress and appearance than she had any idea of. It was as well for her comfort, that she was ignorant of it, and that she did not hear eleven different young ladies assure each other, "She must have sent away to the city for those flowers."

Her uncle and aunts were exceedingly proud of her, and so was Pen. In fact, the latter informed several persons whom she knew, "She's my cousin Susie, and she's the prettiest girl there is here; but I don't believe I shall look much like her when I grow up."

Squire King asked her why not, when she told him, and was at once informed, —

"Susie's never been freckled, and mine won't ever come off. They go away round to the back of my neck. Most all the girls here have got 'em, but they don't amount to any thing."

"Freckles, or girls either," laughed the squire. "But, Pen, does your cousin play the piano?"

"Of course she does, only we haven't any, and so she's learned how to spin. She can crochet, but I showed her how to heel a stocking, and so did aunt Judith."

"I'm sure she can," remarked Mrs. King. "I'll go and ask her myself."

That was not until the party had been in full operation for some time; and quite a number were wondering what it was best to do next, when Mrs. King led Susie to the piano. Several of the local musicians had already done their duty by it, and Susie had consented without a thought of hesitation. She heard a remark as she passed one young lady who had barely missed the outer line of Mrs. King's list of invitations: —

"The flowers are real, and she's pretty enough, but she's too young to play well. They're paying her too much attention, I think."

If there was one thing that Susie loved better than another, it was music, and her teachers had done their duty by her. The moment her fingers touched the keys, they felt entirely at home, and sent back word to her that they would play any thing she could remember. Then they went right on, and convinced every pair of ears within hearing that they were skilfully correct about it.

"I declare!" exclaimed Vosh Stebbins to the little knot around him, "she can play the piano better than she can skate, and that's saying a good deal."

The young folks in two of the farther rooms were playing forfeits, and missed the music, but the promenaders all stood still for a few minutes and listened. It was just like the flowers. Nobody else had brought any thing quite so nice, and there was danger that Susie would be unpopular. As it was, she had no sooner risen from the piano than Squire King announced that supper was ready. Vosh had not known that it was so near, and was compelled to see Adonijah Bunce offer Susie his arm, and lead her into the refreshment-room. He felt that he had made the first real blunder of the evening, but he was wrong about it. Adonijah was so agitated over his success, that he spilled some scalding hot coffee down his left leg, and trod on Susie's toes in consequence. He made her exclaim, "Oh, mercy!" and he made as much blood go into his own face as it could possibly hold at the moment when he said "Golly!" and bit his tongue for it.

There was promenading during all the supper-time, and some music, because the dining-room would not hold them all at once; but, as fast as the young people finished and came out, they set more vigorously at work to enjoy themselves. It was right there that the young people of Benton Valley began

to forgive Susie Hudson for her skating and her
flowers and her music, and for being a city girl.
She went into every thing with such heartiness, that
even Adonijah Bunce began to feel as happy as his
left leg would let him.   Still he was the only young
fellow there who could say that he had poured hot
coffee on himself, if that could be called distinction.
Vosh Stebbins had seen him do it, and had been
more at ease ever since.

Squire King and his wife were in tremendous good
spirits about their party, and they had a right to be.
Aunt Judith herself told them it was the nicest
gathering of young folks that there had ever been in
Benton ; and Pen enjoyed it so much, that at last
she leaned up against Mrs. Keyser on the sitting-
room lounge, and went fast asleep.

It was all over at last, and the guests went home.
Sleigh-load after sleigh-load was packed, and went
jingling away.   The near-by residents marched off
as they had come, except that some young men had
more to take care of, and some young ladies had
other young gentlemen than their own brothers.
Pen went to sleep again in the sleigh, and her father
lifted her out and carried her into the house ; and
the moment she waked up she remarked, —

"He gave me a whole paper of candy, Susie, and
it filled my muff so I couldn't get my hands in."

That had been Squire King's work, and her mother
responded, —

"You're going to bed now, and so is Susie. No candy till morning."

At that very moment Mrs. Stebbins was saying to Vosh, —

"I'm glad we're home again, but we've had a good time. She did look well in them flowers, and she just can play the piano; and you got along first-rate, Lavawjer; and I'm glad you let Nijah Bunce see her in to supper, and wasn't round in the way at no time." She had more to say; but it was a very late bed-time, and she had to put off saying it.

CHAPTER XVII.

THE SNOW-FORT.

THERE was a large amount of conversation performed in Benton Valley the day following the party at Squire King's. It began before breakfast. In some sleeping-rooms it began before people were out of bed. It went on all over the village; and the whole affair was discussed at the drug-store, and in the blacksmith-shop, and at the tavern. It is safe to say that every thing that could be said was said; and the unanimous verdict was, that the party had been a success. So had Susie Hudson been, and she was not omitted from a single description of the company. As for Adonijah Bunce, he obtained some liniment of his mother without telling her just where he had been standing when he spilt the coffee. Susie knew where he stepped next; but she was not very lame, and felt kindly towards Adonijah.

Vosh came over pretty early in the forenoon to see Port and Corry upon a matter of some importance.

"Snow-fort!" exclaimed Porter Hudson a little dignifiedly. "Don't you think we're a little too old for that?"

"Not if it's finished up in the way they began it," replied Vosh. "They went at it after school, and I guess they must have finished it this morning. We'll have the biggest game of draw you ever got into, and we can keep it up all day."

"I'm in for it," said Corry; but Port had really never seen any snow citadels, nor had he been in any game of draw. He remembered reading that Benedict Arnold mounted his cannon on a snow-fort, the better to pepper Quebec, but he had a dim and small opinion of such matters. Still it was a promise of fun, and he went right along. The weather had been growing milder for two days, and that Saturday morning the sun had actually risen with yellow in his face. Deacon Farnham had predicted a change in the weather yet to come, and said something very deep about sap in trees, and of how he must watch it. Port could not imagine any method of watching the movements of sap in trees, or any reason for caring how it moved. He was now thinking with increasing interest about snowballs and their uses, for Vosh explained to him the proposed game of "draw" as they went down the hill.

"Three to one is fair odds," he said; "and, if a fellow gets hit, he changes sides. I've seen a fort

drawn so full, they had half of 'em to sit down ; and
the last fellow out had no chance to pick up a snowball, for dodging what they gave him.   It's just so if
there's only one left in the fort.   He can hardly
show his head without having one of his ears filled.
The snow'll pack first-rate just now.   It'll stick
together, but it won't make too hard a ball.   Wet
snow'll pack into a wad that stings, and it'll do dam-
age too, sometimes."

Port remembered something about that from even
his small experience in the city.   He had paid for a
pane of glass once.

The boys of Benton Village had snowballed a great
deal that winter.   They had grown to be pretty ex-
pert marksmen, and their dodging qualities had improved.   They had even made snow breastworks two
or three times ; but their ambition in that direction
had recently been stimulated by a picture in one of
the illustrated papers.   All hands had agreed that
the right kind of a fort had never yet been built
upon that green, and that it was time to have one.
Snow was plentiful, and so were shovels ; and, so
long as it was play, there were boys enough to do
the work, hard as it might be.   They made it square,
and the walls were nearly two feet thick.   They were
so high that the shorter boys complained that only
their heads came above it.

It made them all the safer in a game of draw, and

they could throw nearly as well. The fort was not finished on Friday evening, because so many of the leading boys were to be at Mrs. King's party; but, by the time Vosh and his two neighbors got there Saturday forenoon, they were beginning to draw for sides.

"There's just twenty-four of us, Vosh," said Adonijah Bunce. "That's six for the fort, and eighteen for the field, to begin on. Draw your cut now, and see where you belong."

"There," said Vosh as he pulled a straw from the hand extended to him: "where does it send me?"

"Into the fort. I'm outside. — Now, Corry, you and Port."

They drew, and discovered that they also were outsiders, under Capt. Bunce; while Vosh was to command the fort as long as the sharp practice should let him stay there.

"It begins to look as if it were going to amount to something," said Port to himself, when it was explained to him that none of his crowd could go in beyond a certain line about forty feet from the snowy wall, nor retreat beyond another line twice as distant.

Vosh and his garrison of five privates were inside the fort in a twinkling, and there were piles of snowballs there ready for use. So there were along the lines of the attacking forces; and the shout of "All ready!" had hardly been uttered, before the missiles began to fly.

Porter Hudson was determined to do himself credit, and at once dashed up to the line, throwing as he went.

"Pick him," said Vosh to his men, and the next instant all their heads came in sight at once. Capt. Bunce's force was well enough disciplined, and their volley at those heads was prompt; but six balls came straight for Porter Hudson. He dodged two, and one missed him widely; but another lodged in his neck, another came spat against his waistband, and the sixth took off his hat.

"Called in!" shouted Vosh, and Port belonged to the garrison. So, in a few moments more, did three other of Capt. Bunce's marksmen; but he had played draw before, and was beginning to wake up. He divided his men, scattering them all around the fort, and Port's next experience came to him in that way. A random ball came over the opposite wall, and landed in the middle of his back. He was again in the field, but his place was taken by the young man who was learning to play the flute. Standing still a moment to warm his hands, and whistle, a pellet thrown by Corry Farnham had broken on his nose, and spoiled the music. The fun grew fast and furious, and the fort was steadily gaining, until Vosh Stebbins made a blunder. He saw somebody walking along on the sidewalk beyond the green, but did not notice who they were till Corry remarked, —

"Halloo! Aunt Judith and Susie. Guess they're going to see Mrs. King. Morning call, eh ?"

The attention of Capt. Bunce was drawn in the same direction by a youth who said to him, —

"There's that young lady from New York. See her ?"

Adonijah turned to do so, and stood still long enough for Vosh Stebbins to make a perfect and undodging mark of him. The ball was a hard one, and it struck precisely upon the liniment, the spot where the coffee had been. Nijah jumped, but he was a drawn man ; and so, alas for the fortunes of that fort! was Capt. Stebbins. He too stood still too long ; and he was bare-headed now, looking around for his cap, and rubbing his red right ear, where a globe of well-packed snow had landed forcibly.

Susie and her aunt stood still for some minutes, watching the game, without the least idea that they had any thing to do with the exchange of leaders. They were indeed on their way to Mrs. King's ; but aunt Judith had other errands, or she would have let that ceremony wait.

Vosh had been studying war all that morning, and he was hardly among the outsiders before he tried a new plan of attack.

"Now, boys," he shouted, "you do as I tell you. Take the corners, — half of us against the corner this way, and half against the opposite corner; and they'll have to kind o' bunch up to throw back, and you're bound to hit somebody. Make a lot of balls, and get good and ready, and we'll empty that fort."

It worked very much in that way. The defenders of the fort were drawn carelessly towards the corners, under a raking fire. The pellets flew over among them thick and fast; and in less than three minutes Coriolanus Farnham stood alone, the entire garrison of the frosty fortress. He stood in a bending posture, against the inner face of a wall, while all around him flew the snowballs that were searching for him. He was a forlorn hope, but he meant to stick it out. He even rose suddenly to return the volleys with a solitary shot. He threw, but so did twenty-three assailants from various directions; and Nijah Bunce had waited, with a knowledge of his whereabouts.

"Called out!" shouted Vosh. "What are you rubbing for, Corry?"

"Got hit all over."

"Game's up," said Nijah. "Now, boys, we'll choose over again."

"Not till I've had a rest," said Corry; and Port remarked, —

"I'll hold on. My arm's too lame to throw another ball."

So was every other arm among them, by the time they had emptied that fort again; but it was voted the best snowballing of the season.

CHAPTER XVIII.

THE SUGAR-BUSH AND THE BEAR.

THE winter days went swiftly on, with constant repetitions of chess and fireside comfort in evenings, and snowballing, skating, sleigh-rides, and other fun whenever the circumstances permitted. There were frequent and long letters from the South, and other and shorter letters from the city. A pretty steady comparison of climates could be made from time to time, and there was no small interest in that. Susie and Port became as well known in Benton Village as if they had been residents, and at least a dozen of the young ladies they knew had learned to skate. Old Miss Turner, the dressmaker, tried it; but she told her friends that she tore her dress and spoiled her bonnet for nothing, and she wouldn't bump the back of her head in that way any more.

"Aunt Sarah!" suddenly exclaimed Susie one afternoon, when she had just finished reading a letter from Florida, "mother says she is as well as ever, and that, now spring is coming" —

248

"Spring! Why, it's hardly beyond the end of February yet. The winter'll hold on till April, and maybe till nigh the end of it."

"Well, away down there they've had real warm weather."

"Now, Susie, you sit right down and write to her that the snow's three feet deep on a level, and she mustn't dream of running the risk of her health in coming North till May."

"Spring'll come earlier in the city than it will up here, aunt Sarah. You can't think how I want to see her."

Port was listening, and he drew a long breath; but he said nothing, and looked very hard out of the window at the endless reaches of snow. They were there, but the long cold "snap" was unmistakably over. It was after supper, that very evening, that Deacon Farnham remarked to his wife, —

"Sarah, the sun's been pretty warm on the trees, and the sap'll be running. I must be getting ready. I mean to have the biggest kind of a sugaring this year."

"I'm glad of it, Joshua. It'll be something for the young folks too. I'm half afraid Susie's beginning to be homesick."

"Nonsense," said aunt Judith; "but of course she wants to see her mother. She and Port are doin' something or other all the while. It's been just one jump with 'em, and they've had a good time. They read a good deal, too; and Port shot two more rabbits only yesterday, and carried 'em over to Mrs. Stebbins."

The city cousins had indeed had a good time; but they did not tell anybody how glad they were to see the sun climbing higher, and to feel sure that spring was nearer.

The increasing sun-power was settling and packing the drifts; and the bitter nights were all that witnessed, for about a week, to the remaining strength of the winter. The sap began to run, as the deacon said it would, and he was fully ready for it. His sugar harvest was to be gathered among the maple-trees on the south-lying slope, near the spot where he had done most of his chopping. There were trees there of the right sort, in great plenty, — great towering old fellows that could well afford to lose a little sap.

"Judith," said Mrs. Farnham, while her husband was at the barn loading his wood-sleigh with the things he would need at the sugar-bush, "we must have the sewing society meet at our house right in sugaring-time."

"It'll be the very thing to do, and I'm glad you thought of it. Only it'll take a good deal of sugar to sweeten some of 'em."

There was more to be said; but Port and Susie

had no share in the discussion, for they hurried out to the sleigh, and were quickly on their way to the woods. They had already learned that a hundred tall maples, more or less, with holes bored into their sides, and with wooden "spiles" driven into the holes, were thereby transformed into a "bush."

The deacon made the boys leave their guns at home, as he had work for them to do; but Vosh joined them when they passed his house, and he carried his double-barrel on his shoulder. He was laughed at a little, but he said there was no telling when he might find a use for it.

It was a bright and sunny day, but there had been no real thaw as yet. The crust had settled with the snow, and was still firm enough for the workers to walk from tree to tree.

The first business was to tap as many as the deacon thought he could attend to; and the boys had enough to do in carrying from the sleigh the wooden troughs, and placing them where they would catch the steady drip, drip, from the sap-spiles.

"They'll fill pretty fast," said the deacon. "We've got some evening collecting before us, or I'm mistaken. We must have some kettles up as soon as we can."

He and Vosh and the hired man went right at it, and the deacon declared that he would have two more hands from the village the next day. Susie and Pen went with them, and stood watching the process.

"It's easy enough," said Pen, as she saw them struggling with one of the great iron kettles.

Two strong forked stakes were driven down in convenient places, at about eight feet apart. A stout pole was laid across each pair of stakes, resting in the forks. A kettle was swung upon each cross-pole in due season, but only three had been brought that morning. Then all was ready for building a fire under the kettle, and beginning to make sugar.

"Won't the snow melt under it?" asked Susie. "Won't it put out the fire?"

"You'll see," said Vosh. "Of course the snow melts on top, and sinks, and we keep pitching on bark and stuff, and the ashes are there. The water runs off through the snow, and all the stuff gets packed hard, and'll bear as much fire as you can build on it. It makes a cake, and freezes nights, and those cakes'll be the last things around here that melt in spring."

He was aching to get a bucket of sap into that first kettle, and a fire under it, so he could show her how it worked; but the other kettles had to be set up first. It was well that there should be enough of them to take the sap as it came, so that nobody need be tempted to throw cold sap into boiling sirup at the wrong time. A barrel was brought up afterwards, to hold any surplus that a kettle was not ready for.

While the workers at the sugar-bush were pushing forward their preparations, Susie and Port were learning a great deal about maple-sugar processes. They could not help remembering all they knew about other kinds of sugar. At the same time there was much activity at the farmhouse. Aunt Judith put on her things, as soon as she could spare the time for it, and went over to consult with Mrs. Stebbins. Then they both came back to see Mrs. Farnham; and all three wrapped up, and made the quickest kind of a walk to the village. They made several short calls separately, and, when they came together again, Mrs. Stebbins announced the result triumphantly, —

"We've set the ball a-rollin'. Elder Evans'll give it out in meeting this evening. All the rest of 'em'll send word, and he'll give it out again on Sunday. If we don't have your house full next Tuesday, I'm all out in my count."

Sugar-making in a large "bush" is not a business to be finished up in a day or two. The weather grew better and better for it, and Deacon Farnham's extra "hands" were kept at it most industriously. Tuesday came, and Mrs. Stebbins was not at all out in her count. The house began to look lively even before noon. Squire King and his wife came just after dinner, and their sleigh could not have held one more passenger. It went right back for some more. It was curious, too, considering that everybody knew all about sugaring. Old or young, hardly any of them were contented until they had paid a visit to the "bush," and drunk some sap. Some of the younger people seemed very much inclined to stay there.

"There won't be any great amount of sewing done for the poor heathen," remarked one good old lady, with a lump of maple-sugar in one hand, and a kruller in the other. "What's more, all their appetites'll be spiled, and they won't enjoy eatin' any thing."

Some afterwards seemed really to have suffered that injury, but not the majority, by any means. The later arrivals, especially, came hungry. All the latter part of that afternoon seemed to be one pretty steady-going dinner or supper. The ladies of the society poured right out into the kitchen to help aunt Judith, till she begged that no more should come at once than could stand around the stove.

It was well that there should be a sugar-bush, or some sort of excitement, to keep a part of that gathering out of doors. The house was full enough at all times; and before sunset the knots of merry people scattered around among the maple-trees and kettles discovered why Vosh Stebbins had persisted in carrying his gun out there every day since the work began.

Vosh had dreamed of such a thing, and had been almost half afraid of it; but he had hoped in his heart that it might come, and the peaceful course of events had disappointed him. He was getting ready to start for the house that day, gun and all, when he heard somebody scream, away up near the farthest clump of sugar-trees, —

"Bear, bear, bear! There's a bear drinking sap!"

Ever so many voices were raised at once to announce to everybody the arrival of that ferocious wild animal, recently waked from his winter's nap. They told of the dreadful thing he was doing, and suggested other dreadful things that he might do. He might eat up the society.

"They generally come at night," said the deacon calmly, "but they are very apt to visit a sugar-bush. They're fond of sap."

"Where's Susie? Where's Pen?" exclaimed Vosh. Then he remembered that they and a whole party of village girls were up there near those very trees, and he ran as if his life depended on it.

"Steady, Vosh. Not so fast. I'm a-coming."

There was the deacon panting behind him, axe in hand; and behind him was the hired man with his axe, and away behind him were three or four sturdy farmers following with no better weapons than sled-stakes.

Port and Corry were with the girls, and it had

been a wonder how quickly the last girl and boy to be seen had gotten behind a tree. They were all now peering out for a look at the bear, and Penelope declared of him, —

"He's the largest bear in the world. He's awful!"

Not all of them were where they could see him, and he was making no effort at all to see them, but his offence was that he had come. No doubt but he had been a little scared at first, when the girls began to scream; but he was hungry and thirsty, and he was fond of sap, and he took courage. There were all those troughs ready for him, and he could not think of going away without a good drink.

Besides, the bear could not see that any of those young ladies seemed disposed to come any nearer, and he had not been introduced to one of them. So he overcame any bashfulness, and put his nose into another sap-trough, and it was empty in a twinkling. He served another in the same way, and was going ahead quite contentedly, nearer and nearer the girls that were afraid to run. At least half a dozen were braver, and ran remarkably well towards the kettles. Port and Corry, behind their trees, were longing for all sorts of weapons, when they saw something well worth seeing.

The bear stood still suddenly; for a dark-eyed, plucky-looking boy, with something in his hands, stood right in the way.

"What are you loaded with, Vosh?" shouted the deacon. "Nothing but buckshot? It's risky."

"Buckshot, and two slugs in each barrel."

"That's better. He's turned a little. Take him in the shoulder."

"Bang, bang!" was the reply made by the gun. It was close work, and not many of the leaden missiles wandered from their broad black target.

The bear was mortally wounded, but he instantly gathered his remaining strength for a charge. The furiously angry growl he gave sent a thrill and chill through all the bones of the scattered spectators.

Right past Vosh at that moment sprang the deacon; and he met the bear halfway, like the brave old borderer that he was. He was a master-hand with an axe, and its keen edge fell with a thud squarely between the eyes of the ferocious animal. It sank in as if the bear's head had been the side of a hickory, and there was no need of any second blow.

The bear was dead; and all the sugar makers and eaters could cluster around and make remarks upon him, and praise Vosh Stebbins and the deacon.

"Pen!" exclaimed Susie, "what will his mother say of him now?"

"Why, they'll skin him, and it'll make the beautifullest kind of a buffalo-robe."

Pen was thinking of the bear only; and Vosh had at once reloaded and shouldered his gun, and walked away. He was ready for another bear, but felt pretty sure that none would come. Port and Corry gave up going to the house for guns and coming back again, and all the young ladies seemed to think it must be near supper-time. They carried the news to Mrs. Stebbins, and it was all but provoking that she should take it very much as a matter of course. If any bear came to be killed, it was as natural as life that her boy should kill him. He was a young fellow from whom uncommon things were to be commonly expected.

After the adventure with the bear, the sewing society was a greater success than before. It went right on until late into the evening, but the success of it was not in the sewing that was done. The only heathen for whom much was accomplished was probably the bear himself.

Susie Hudson said to her brother at last, "I don't care, Port, it beats a city party all to pieces. There's ever so much more real enjoyment. I want to live in the country."

"Oh, well, I like it in winter. It's well enough. You've been out here in summer too."

"It's twice as good then."

"No, Susie, it can't be. It must be all hard work in summer. But think of the fun we've had!"

She did; and late in the evening Vosh Stebbins stepped up to her, and whispered, —

"May I see you home? The cutter's waiting at the door. All the rest are getting ready to start."

"I've got to say good-by to them all, I suppose."

"Go round and say it now. I don't want to sleigh-ride anybody else. They've all got company."

That was the reason why, a little afterwards, Vosh Stebbins's mother could not find him. He and Susie were jingling over the snow behind the sorrel colt, and it was a long way home before they returned to the house.

CHAPTER XIX.

THE FLOOD AND THE END.

It was well for all who were fond of sleighing, to make the best use of their time. A great many people had had enough, and were even eager to see the snow depart. There was a great deal of it to go, and the weather took an unexpected part in the matter. The sun came out with a power that had in it something peculiar, and made all human beings feel drowsy, heavy, listless, and disposed to take boneset-tea. The older they were, the more black and bitter was the boneset they called for; and aunt Judith manufactured some uncommonly good root-beer to go with it. So far as the young people were concerned, the root-beer went much more rapidly than the boneset.

Then arrived two whole days of warm and heavy rain; and, when the sun came out again, he had an altered landscape to look down upon. All the hill-sides were streaming with torrents of water, and

260

every hollow was a pond. The roads were channels of temporary rivulets, and the river in the valley had swollen until its fetters were breaking. The ice in the mill-pond cracked and lifted until the water broke out over the dam. That relieved the pressure for a few hours, until the huge cakes of ice got in a hurry, and began to climb upon each others' shoulders. They rapidly built up a dam of their own, right on top of the old one, and the water sent back up stream for more ice. As fast as the new supplies came down, they were heaped up, right and left and centre; and no engineer could have done the work better, so far as increasing the size of the mill-pond was concerned. It grew tremendously, and the sun toiled at the snowbanks on the hillsides, all along the banks of that river, away up into the mountains, to send down more snow-water for the big spread in Benton Valley.

"Sarah," said Deacon Farnham at about the middle of the second forenoon, "if this thing keeps on, it'll drown out the village."

"Has the water got there yet?" she asked. "Is it rising?"

"Rising! Guess it is. I'll hitch up the team after dinner, and we'll go and take a look at it."

When Pen and Corry came home at noon, they reported that school was dismissed for the day; and Pen explained it, —

"She said the Flood was coming again, but I don't believe it is."

"Not Noah's Flood," said her father; "but enough might come to carry away the schoolhouse. I can't say what they're going to do about it."

The story Vosh told at home brought Mrs. Stebbins over after dinner, and there was a full sleigh-load driven down to see the sights.

Susie and Port were to have one more experience of winter life in the country, and it was one they would not have missed for any thing. The mill-pond was away below the village, and there was another up towards Cobbleville that was said to be nearly as badly off. As the water had risen, it had set back and back, until now the low-lying lands were a great lake with houses and barns sticking up from it. Deacon Farnham drove on down towards the village, and all the tongues in the sleigh grew more and more silent. Aunt Judith had already told all there was to tell about the great flood when she was a girl, and when they had to live without flour or meal. The story sounded much more real now, for the first man they met said to them, —

"If the ice goes on packing up there at the dam, the mill and all will break away before midnight."

"Are they trying to do any thing to loosen the pack?" asked Vosh.

"They can't get at it to pick at it, and it's wuth

any man's life to try. The water's in the main street now."

"What if the upper dam should give way?" asked the deacon.

"Well, if the ice there and the dam should give way all at once, and come down in a heap, there wouldn't be much left of Benton."

They drove on down the road to the right, towards what had been the lower level of the coasting-hill, where the sleds darted out upon the pond. They could see the whole thing now, and the long ridge of ice with the flood surging and rising against it, and filling up every lower place with fresh material. The water was still pouring over the pack at the upper dam, the deacon said, or no more ice and snow would be coming down.

"Mr. Farnham!" suddenly exclaimed Vosh Stebbins, "I wish I had money enough to pay for a keg of blasting-powder."

"What for, Vosh?"

"Don't you see? You can get to the second floor of the mill, right across those logs. If a keg of powder could be shoved out on the pack, and left there with a slow-match burning, I could get back before it went off."

"I'll pay for the powder," said the deacon as he turned his team towards the village, and Mrs. Stebbins gasped, —

"O Vosh! Lavawjer!"

She sat still, and looked a little white for a moment, and then the color came to her face, and there was a sort of flash in her eyes as she said slowly and steadily, —

"Just you try it on. Your father would have done it any day. Levi Stebbins was a soldier, and he never flinched any thing in all his life."

"Joshaway," said aunt Judith with a bit of a tremor in her voice, "I want to pay for that powder myself. He can buy two kegs if he needs 'em."

The water was nearly a foot deep in front of Rosenstein's store when the sleigh came splashing along. The whole village was boiling with excitement, in spite of the fact that the flood was all of ice-water.

"Powder? Going to blow up dot ice?" said Mr. Rosenstein doubtfully; but he hurried to bring out a keg of it, and a long line of fuze.

"Now, Vosh. No time to lose. You mustn't run any needless risk, but I believe you can do it. I'll go as far as into the mill with you."

"Joshua," said Mrs. Farnham, "will he need help? His weight's a good deal lighter than yours."

"We'll see about it when we get there. That pack has got to be broken: so has the one at the upper dam."

They were once more on the hill-road, and nearing

the point of danger. Great piles of saw-logs, ready for the saw-mill, had accumulated on the slope between the mill and what was now the shore; and already quite a number of adventurers had crossed upon them to the building itself, and back again. Not a soul had cared to remain more than a minute, and none had ventured beyond.

"Go, Joshua," said Mrs. Farnham. "He'll need advice, if he doesn't need any thing else."

Corry took the reins, and his father and Vosh stepped out. There were thirty or forty men and boys standing around and watching the flood, and all were eager to know what was coming; but the answers given them had a short, gruff sound, as if uttered by somebody too much in earnest to talk.

"Right along, Vosh," said the deacon. "The logs are firm enough."

So they were, and it was easy to climb through an open window into the second story of the mill. Through all the lower floor the water was rushing and gurgling, and the building shook all over as if it were chilly.

An opposite window was reached, and there before them was the ice-pack. Only at one point, beyond the centre, was there any water going over it; and it seemed only too strong and solid.

"As far out as you can, Vosh," said the deacon. "Put it into a hole of some kind, if you can."

Without a word of comment or reply, the brave boy crept through the window, and let himself down upon the ice, and the keg was handed him.

"Use the whole length of the fuze," said the deacon. "You'll have time enough."

"Mr. Farnham," said Vosh, "you go back right away, now."

"I don't know but what it's my duty. Do yours quick, Vosh."

He was every way disposed to obey that suggestion. The roar of the waters, the strange sensation of the presence of great peril, and even the idea that so many people were looking at him, made the situation one from which he was in a hurry to get away. Nearly in the middle of the pack he came to a deep crevice between the heaps of glimmering ice, and into it he lowered his little barrel of explosive meal. He had made it all ready, fixing the end of the fuze in its proper place, and now he led the line back over comparatively dry ice.

"Nothing to put it out," he muttered; "and they said it was water-proof, anyhow."

A stream of people, on foot and in sleighs, had followed that undertaking from the moment when the news of it began to buzz around the village, and a full hundred had now gathered on the slope opposite the mill. They saw Vosh Stebbins scratch a match on his coat-sleeve, and stoop down; and then they saw him turn, and walk swiftly away towards the mill.

"It's all right, deacon!" he shouted. "She's a-burning!"

"Come on, Vosh. Hurry up. I just couldn't go ashore till you got back."

Vosh replied with a ringing laugh that had a world of excitement in it. He followed the deacon back through the mill, and across the perilous bridge of floating logs; and there on the shore stood Susie Hudson, and her aunts, and his mother, but Penelope was the only one who said any thing.

"Vosh," she asked, "did you lose all your powder and your string?"

"Guess I have," replied he; and then it was Adonijah Bunce who remarked,—

"Didn't quite do it, did ye?"

"Hold on a minute," said Mr. Farnham. "It was a long fuze."

It seemed as if everybody held their breaths till it must hurt them; but, just when they could not do it any longer, a great sheet of smoke and flame shot up from the middle of the ice-pack. It was followed by a dull, heavy report, and by flying fragments of ice.

Had it accomplished any thing?—that was the question in all minds; but it was only a moment before there was another crash, and another. The barrier had been blown away to such a thinness that the pressure from above was sufficient to break it through. The flood rushed forward into the widening channel with a surge and a plunge, and away went the river again, roaring down its half-deserted bed below. More of the cakes of ice to the right and left, now no longer wedged and self-supporting, were swiftly torn away, and the gap so opened could not be closed again.

"I just knew he'd do it," said Mrs. Stebbins proudly, as the round of cheers died away after the explosion and crash. "His father would ha' done it."

There were plenty to congratulate Vosh; but he and the rest got into the sleigh again, and drove back towards the village. Even before they reached it, the waters were manifestly receding a little, and, when they again stopped in front of Mr. Rosenstein's store, it was pretty well understood that the first peril was over.

"Now for the pack at the upper dam!" shouted the deacon. "It's safe to make a hole in it, now our pack is broken. — I want to pay for that powder, Mr. Rosenstein. I was in such a hurry, I forgot it."

"Dot's joost vot I did," replied the merchant. "You bays for no powder for dot boy. He safe de village. I deals not in pork."

There was a cheer for Mr. Rosenstein; and a

dozen men set off towards the upper dam with more powder, and a new idea.

"We have done enough for one day," said Deacon Farnham after he had seen that squad set out. "We can afford to go home. — Mrs. Stebbins, you and Vosh can take dinner with us, and Susie and Port can read their letters."

All were entirely willing, and the team headed for home as if they were conscious of having done something for the public good. The village post-office was kept in Mr. Rosenstein's store, and that was one reason why the letters had been received in such an hour of excitement. They were not read until after the arrival at the farmhouse, for every one in that sleigh was looking back into the valley to see whether or not the flood was visibly subsiding. Even after they reached the house, Vosh said he felt as if he were about to hear the explosion at the upper dam. He did not hear it; but the ice there was blown open, nevertheless, and the river had a fair chance to carry all its surplus down stream, and melt it up instead of making dams of it.

Porter Hudson was the first to tear open an envelope.

"Susie!" he shouted almost instantly, "mother's got home."

Her fingers were busy with her own letter for a moment, and then she turned to Mrs. Farnham.

"Aunt Sarah!"

"O Susie! I know what you mean. They want you at home."

"Yes," said aunt Judith, "I suppose we've got to say good-by to 'em pretty soon."

"And there's no winter at all in the city," said Port. "No snow to be seen, and some of the buds are beginning to show."

The letters had a powerful effect upon all the gathering around that dinner-table; and Pen thought she had settled the difficulty, or nearly so, when she broke a long silence with, —

"They might just as well all come up here and live. There's room for 'em all, and it's ever so much better than the city is."

There was no immediate haste called for, but winter was over. Word came from the village in the morning, that the flood was going down fast, and the mill was entirely safe, and that everybody was talking about the feat performed by Vosh Stebbins. It looked as if Mr. Farnham's part of it was a little neglected, and Pen remarked with some jealousy, — '

"Father got the powder, and all Vosh did was to touch it off."

Everybody seemed to feel blue that evening, for some reason; and the thaw carried away almost all the snow there was left, with hardly a remark being made about it. The fire in the sitting-room burned

low, and no fresh logs were heaped upon it. Susie
sat in front of it, and remembered a summer day
when she had seen nothing there but polished and-
irons, and branches of fennel.

"Port," said Corry almost mournfully, "I do hope
you've had a good time. We all want you to come
again."

"Good time ! Tell you what, Corry, I won't come
up here unless you'll come and visit us in the city.
I've been thinking over lots of things I could show
you and Pen. I've had the biggest kind of a time."

"You must come up some time in summer," said
aunt Judith. "The country is beautiful then. Better fishing, hunting — all sorts of fun."

"I guess there isn't any thing better than winter
fun," said Susie thoughtfully. "I do like the country at any time of the year."

Vosh Stebbins and his mother also sat in front
of their sitting-room fireplace, and were uncommonly
still and sober.

"Mother," said he at last, "I've had the greatest
winter I ever did have. There's been any amount
of fun in it, but seems to me there's been a good
deal more."

"Yes," said his mother, "they've been right good
company, and I'm real sorry to hev 'em go ; but it's
time they went, and her mother's health's come
back to her. She's one of the best of women, I

haven't the least doubt in the world. I never seen a girl I took to more'n I hev to Susie Hudson, and I hope she and Port'll come up here again; and I've been a-findin' out how much it'll cost to hev you go to college, and you've got to jest study up and go."

"Mother!" That was all he could say; for his mind had been playing chess with that problem since he did not know exactly when, and he had not dared to speak of it.

One week later the Farnham and Stebbins farm-houses felt smaller and lonelier, and Penelope teased for a pen and ink, remarking, —

"If I write to Susie right away, it may get there almost as soon as she does, and she won't have to wait for it to come."

The rest of the family and their neighbors had their hands full of spring work, and had no time to think much of their recent visitors; but their visitors were thinking of them. A lady and gentleman in a city home were listening to prolonged and full accounts of their children's winter in the country, and every now and then the gentleman exclaimed, —

"Vosh Stebbins again!" At the end of it all, he said to his wife, —

"My dear, did you know that youngsters of that kind were scarce? I must keep an eye on him. Susie says he's to have an education. Got a good beginning for one now, I should say. If he should go straight, there's no telling what he might do. He can graduate from college into my office, if he wishes to. I knew his father, and his mother's as good as gold."

"Hurrah!" shouted Port. "Then Vosh can kill his bears in the city. How'd you like that, Susie? I'd like it."

Susie only turned to her mother, and asked, —

"What do you think, mother?"

"I? Oh, we will have plenty of time to think it over. We can go up there and visit, and we can have them down here."

Nevertheless Vosh did go to college, and he did pass from it to Mr. Hudson's law-office; and it is true, to this day, that nobody can tell what he will do, he is doing so much and so well.

∏ Trieste

Trieste Publishing has a massive catalogue of classic book titles. Our aim is to provide readers with the highest quality reproductions of fiction and non-fiction literature that has stood the test of time. The many thousands of books in our collection have been sourced from libraries and private collections around the world.

The titles that Trieste Publishing has chosen to be part of the collection have been scanned to simulate the original. Our readers see the books the same way that their first readers did decades or a hundred or more years ago. Books from that period are often spoiled by imperfections that did not exist in the original. Imperfections could be in the form of blurred text, photographs, or missing pages. It is highly unlikely that this would occur with one of our books. Our extensive quality control ensures that the readers of Trieste Publishing's books will be delighted with their purchase. Our staff has thoroughly reviewed every page of all the books in the collection, repairing, or if necessary, rejecting titles that are not of the highest quality. This process ensures that the reader of one of Trieste Publishing's titles receives a volume that faithfully reproduces the original, and to the maximum degree possible, gives them the experience of owning the original work.

We pride ourselves on not only creating a pathway to an extensive reservoir of books of the finest quality, but also providing value to every one of our readers. Generally, Trieste books are purchased singly - on demand, however they may also be purchased in bulk. Readers interested in bulk purchases are invited to contact us directly to enquire about our tailored bulk rates. Email: customerservice@triestepublishing.com

You May Also Like

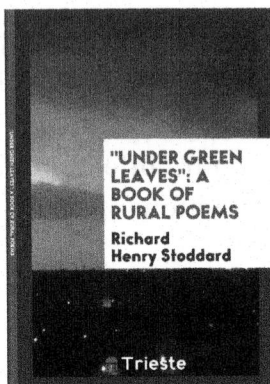

ISBN: 9780649727193
Paperback: 122 pages
Dimensions: 6.14 x 0.26 x 9.21 inches
Language: eng

"Under Green Leaves": A Book of Rural Poems

Richard Henry Stoddard

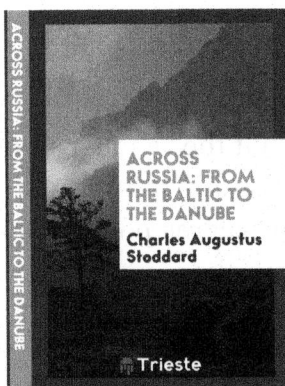

ISBN: 9780649036776
Paperback: 306 pages
Dimensions: 6.14 x 0.64 x 9.21 inches
Language: eng

Across Russia: From the Baltic to the Danube

Charles Augustus Stoddard

www.triestepublishing.com

You May Also Like

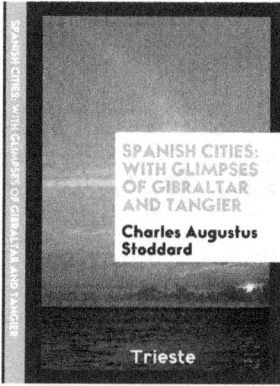

Spanish Cities: With Glimpses of Gibraltar and Tangier

Charles Augustus Stoddard

ISBN: 9780649709809
Paperback: 290 pages
Dimensions: 6.14 x 0.61 x 9.21 inches
Language: eng

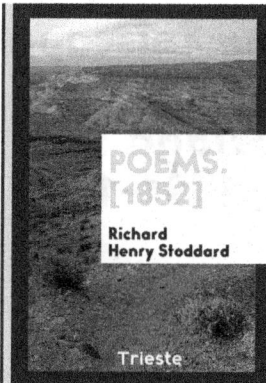

Poems. [1852]

Richard Henry Stoddard

ISBN: 9780649673186
Paperback: 142 pages
Dimensions: 6.0 x 0.30 x 9.0 inches
Language: eng

www.triestepublishing.com

You May Also Like

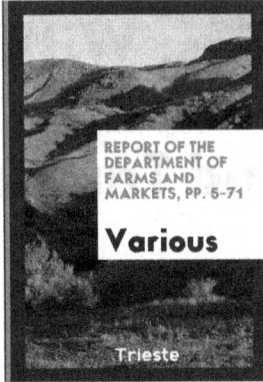

Report of the Department of Farms and Markets, pp. 5-71

Various

ISBN: 9780649333158
Paperback: 84 pages
Dimensions: 6.14 x 0.17 x 9.21 inches
Language: eng

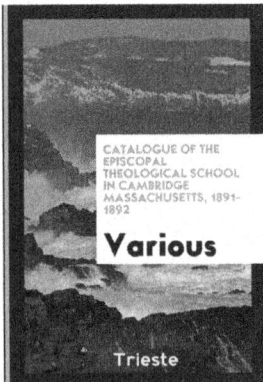

Catalogue of the Episcopal Theological School in Cambridge Massachusetts, 1891-1892

Various

ISBN: 9780649324132
Paperback: 78 pages
Dimensions: 6.14 x 0.16 x 9.21 inches
Language: eng

You May Also Like

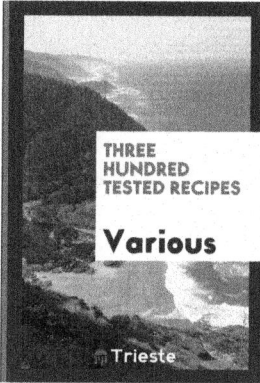

Three Hundred Tested Recipes

Various

ISBN: 9780649352142
Paperback: 88 pages
Dimensions: 6.14 x 0.18 x 9.21 inches
Language: eng

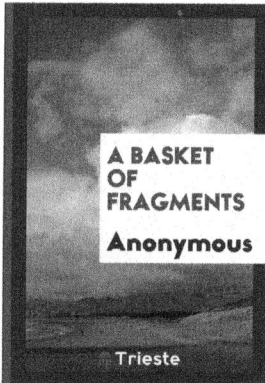

A Basket of Fragments

Anonymous

ISBN: 9780649419418
Paperback: 108 pages
Dimensions: 6.14 x 0.22 x 9.21 inches
Language: eng

Find more of our titles on our website. We have a selection of thousands of titles that will interest you. Please visit

www.triestepublishing.com

Lightning Source UK Ltd.
Milton Keynes UK
UKOW06f0615231017
311485UK00004B/380/P